CULT SHOES

CULT SHOES
Classic and Contemporary Designs

Harriet Walker

MERRELL
LONDON · NEW YORK

Introduction

Paradoxically, the humble shoe is at once one of fashion's most accessible and most exclusive offshoots. We all wear shoes; we all need them. But as far as everyday items go, they are some of the most highly constructed, the most highly designed and, arguably, the most complex.

The labour that goes into the production of a pair of shoes is a vocation unto itself, an artisanal heritage that abides even in some of the loftier labels. The triumvirate of Manolo Blahnik, Jimmy Choo and Christian Louboutin is emblematic of the skill and craftsmanship the discipline demands: despite the introduction of mass production and mass marketing, the footwear greats remain those who work in this traditional and individualistic vein. These venerated shoemakers are the architects of the fashion world, working against gravity and heft, often against reality itself.

If the twentieth century altered sartorial codes irrevocably, in the (literal) loosening of feminine attire and the de-formalizing of occasionwear, then it also shifted the focus of an outfit away from merely clothes to include accessories. If anything, this was a shift back to form, as shoes have long been admired as *objets* above and beyond their practical use. But since the mid-nineteenth century, footwear had not been a focal point; it was rarely even considered as part of an ensemble.

The masters and megastars in this book are some of the most successful in their field. Many have – quite separately from the industry itself – turned footwear into a fashion in its own right. You will read of penthouses and pavements, of high-end and high street, of mainstream and sub-cultures, and you will learn about the sorts of shoes that have facilitated giant leaps for mankind.

Christian Louboutin has quite literally altered the way people view shoes: not simply from above but also from below, to check for that all-important red sole, which he has made his signature. Manolo Blahnik's name, meanwhile, is a synecdoche for refined elegance and in-the-know fashionability. The brand Jimmy Choo has lived on as a company – a highly successful one at that – long after its namesake departed.

Is it any wonder that those who pursue this line of work are some of the most

imaginative in the fashion industry, and that many of them are revered as gods, their brands internationally famous, their names part of the very vernacular of contemporary culture? Shoes hold a special place in our hearts for all the flights of fantasy they have come to embody, but it is their ability to combine the mundane and the magical that keeps us hooked.

In 1272 the Worshipful Company of Cordwainers was formed in London, a livery guild for those who worked in the shoemaking profession. The name derives from 'cordwain' or 'cordovan', a type of goatskin from Cordoba, Spain, from which footwear was traditionally made. While the guild's credentials as a trade body have waned, its cultural bequest is London's – if not the world's – most influential footwear design college, now part of the London College of Fashion but still referred to by its historical name. Designers who trained at Cordwainers include Jimmy Choo and Patrick Cox, and the younger luminaries Camilla Skovgaard, Nicholas Kirkwood and Charlotte Olympia.

While advances in technology and components have had a bearing on how

shoes are made and the way they look, the process of manufacturing footwear is still very close to its roots. Leather is stretched over 'lasts' (foot-shaped moulds usually made from wood or wax), and soles are nailed or glued on. However complex and foreign a finished shoe may look, this process retains that heritage of craft and handiwork that so strongly informs our idea of a good-quality pair of shoes. Salvatore Ferragamo was notorious for keeping each customer's lasts, from Marlene Dietrich's to Ava Gardner's, while Christian Louboutin has an entire room of them, labelled with such names as Loulou de La Falaise and Daphne Guinness.

But the phenomenon of the stand-out shoe or the influential designer is nothing new. Fashion history is littered with events that flag up the importance of footwear. In 1525 Henry VIII's personal shoemaker, Cornelius Johnson, became the first person to make a pair of football boots – although he could hardly have known it – when he attached crude spikes to the soles of the monarch's shoes so that he might enjoy a better grip during outdoor pursuits. Legend has it that one sixteenth-century shoemaker

Above, **left** 'A Roper and a Cordwainer', from the school textbook *Orbis sensualium pictus* (*The Visible World in Pictures*; 1659) by John Amos Comenius.

Above Hyacinthe Rigaud (1659–1743), *Louis XIV, King of France*, 1701, Louvre, Paris. The king is pictured wearing the red heels that were all the rage among the French aristocracy.

The actresses Ava Gardner (left) and Marlene Dietrich, both long-time customers of Salvatore Ferragamo.

from Norwich, John Drakes, saw fit to array himself in the fashion of a noble gentleman, such was his income from his trade. Under the strict etiquette of Versailles, meanwhile, it was frowned on for royals to wear the same pair of shoes twice (apparently Marlene Dietrich never did, either); and when the gilded dream came crashing down in 1793, it was the rebel shoemaker Antoine Simon who took charge of the then Dauphin (the uncrowned Louis XVII).

The reason for the popularity of fashionable footwear is simple: consumers love the objectification of the quotidian. The shoe is as much a status symbol now as it was in the time of Louis XIV, when it was de rigueur for the heels of the aristocracy to be painted red. In 2011 the British Museum in London exhibited a first-century slipper with solid gold on its sole, as part of its show *Afghanistan: Crossroads of the Ancient World*. Treating the feet as ornaments is one of the most ancient and most emphatic ways of proving status: the more money one lavishes on one's feet, the more obvious it is that those feet are not expected to walk very far.

The traditional practice of Chinese foot-binding is often invoked during arguments about high-heeled shoes and their crippling effect (both literally and metaphorically) on women: in the tenth century, girls' feet were bent and broken, and bound into a dainty 5-inch-long (12.5 cm) shape that was supposed to resemble a golden lily. The daintier the foot, the bigger the woman's dowry; the richest of women were not supposed to work or even to walk unaided. Nowadays high-end labels create vertiginous confections that, although not promoted as impossible to walk in, are rarely seen queuing for buses or trotting home after a day in the office.

For centuries heels have been linked with status, not least for their literal stature-boosting qualities, but things came to a head in 2008, a year notorious for its excesses in fashion (the release of Burberry's £13,000 handbag) and in finance (the sudden collapses of Bear Stearns and Lehman Brothers). Stefano Pilati gave his Tribute court shoe, designed for Yves Saint Laurent, a double platform and a 4-inch (10-cm) heel; the smallest heel available in Christian Louboutin's Spring/Summer collection that year was 5½ inches (14 cm); and cosmetic surgeons in Los Angeles began offering toe amputation to ease the pain of wearing these extreme heels. When I dubbed these new mega-stilettos 'taxi-to-table' shoes in an article that year, I had no idea what an enduring motif the shoe as status marker would be.[1]

Nevertheless, modern-day footwear fetishists have strongly bought into these extremes. The more flamboyant the shoe, the better; the higher, the better; all in all, the more obvious, the better. Louboutin's red soles have become not only one of the best marketing tools around (everyone from Oprah Winfrey to Carla Bruni-Sarkozy has revealed the telltale flashes of crimson on the underside of their shoes), but also the easiest way to tell if someone really knows what's what in the world of shoes.

In 1956 Salvatore Ferragamo created a shoe with a carved heel in 18-carat gold, setting his customer back £700. In 1999 a pair of rhinestone-covered ruby-red court shoes that had belonged to Marilyn Monroe sold for £30,760 at Christie's. That year, the Bond Street 'shoe-turier' Gina entered the record book with a pair of alligator-skin mules topped with thirty-six diamonds; the shoes cost £18,000. The shoes in the designer Antonio Berardi's Spring/Summer 1999 collection were made by Manolo Blahnik from 18-carat gold. Each pair was worth almost £6000, and they came with their own security guard. At his Spring/Summer 2000 couture show for Christian Dior, John Galliano had models parade on a mirrored catwalk to flaunt the diamond-strewn undersides of their jewel-encrusted boots. Christian Louboutin has special clients for whom he creates bespoke shoes, and he soled one pair not with his traditional red lacquer but with priceless – and freshly mined – rubies.

In September 2010 the London department store Selfridges unveiled its Shoe Galleries, the largest shoe department in the world, covering 35,000 square feet (3250 sq. m). Bigger than the turbine hall of Tate Modern, the futuristic interior houses more than 5000 pairs of shoes from more than 120 brands. Footwear

Carla Bruni-Sarkozy (wife of the former French president Nicolas Sarkozy) in Louboutin heels, with HRH Prince Charles at the statue of King George VI and Queen Elizabeth on the Mall, London, 18 June 2010.

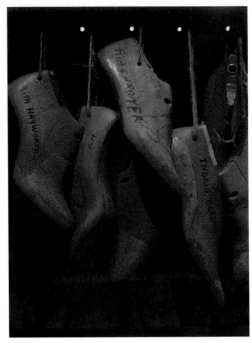

has become an industry dedicated to and founded on hyperbole; while the shoes themselves may be big, so are the amounts of money involved. People are willing to go to great lengths for their feet; it's no coincidence that to be described as 'well-heeled' implies that one has risen to the top of the pile.

The day I agreed to write this book, I fell off some 4-inch platforms and broke my left leg in three places. I was especially astonished because these had previously been my 'comfortable' boots.

Tastes in footwear alter, of course, depending on the climate and the context, just as trends in clothing come and go. Fashion is cyclical, so styles come back at an alarming pace. Spring/Summer 2012, for example, saw the resurgence of the mule shoe, courtesy of catwalk shows from the likes of Louis Vuitton (opposite); only six

months earlier, that style had been decried as naff, or worse, as a 'porn-star shoe'. It was a similar story with the extreme platforms that have come to characterize early twenty-first-century footwear: before their fashionable reincarnation, the only people wearing these styles were those who worked in the adult-entertainment sector.

Shoes owe much to sex. The stiletto heel (from the Italian for 'sharp dagger') as we know it was invented in the 1950s by Roger Vivier, who was among the first to design shoes for Christian Dior. The style promotes perkiness, thrusting out the breasts and bottom, elongating the legs and imbuing the wearer with a somewhat slinkier gait than usual. Japanese geishas wear traditional *geta* shoes – stacked wooden thong sandals – for the same reason: to make them sashay, and to add to their idiosyncratic fragility.

Left Yves Saint Laurent, Tribute sandal in black leather.

Left, bottom Louis Vuitton Merry-Go-Round mule in patent and metallic leather, Spring/Summer 2012.

Bondage and other subcultural influences on shoes became increasingly apparent after Manolo Blahnik reintroduced the stiletto at the end of the 1970s' love affair with wedges and platforms. At first the style had seedy connotations; designers have since played on these, so that buckles, belts and other finishes unashamedly reminiscent of sex-industry accoutrements have been incorporated wholesale into the everyday. A woman in heels is sexy in the sort of caricatured way that a woman in flats can never be. Historically, donning heels meant that a woman was of age, as referred to by Shakespeare through Hamlet's mockery of extreme 'chopine' platforms: blocks of wood attached to the soles of shoes, often 4 or 5 inches (10–12.7 cm) thick (*Hamlet*, II. ii. 426–27).

In 2009, at the Trades Union Congress conference in Liverpool, a motion was tabled that women should not be required to wear heels at work, for reasons of health and safety. There are plenty of people who see high heels as yet another instrument of oppression, one more way in which to impede women practically; they are consequently used figuratively in all sorts of contexts. During the anti-feminist backlash of the 1980s, heels were an essential part of the working woman's wardrobe; during the 1990s, trainer culture arrived and, with it, a new minimalist, sporty elegance. It mirrored exactly a similar shift in the eighteenth century, from the opulent heeled shoes of Louis XIV's reign to the flat slippers worn during the neoclassical revival of the brief Directoire era.

There are high-heel aficionados who claim that they can walk only in heels, employing the 'Jell-O on springs' totter popularized by Marilyn Monroe in *Some Like It Hot*. There are also specialists who assert that high heels cause tendons to shorten and joints to weaken. For my part, I anticipate wearing heels as soon as my broken leg is up to the job once more. Whether you walk a mile in someone else's shoes or your own, this book aims to prove that it's not the destination that matters, but the elegant or extreme, classic or cartoonish mode of transportation that you choose.

1. Harriet Walker, 'Skyscraper Heels: They May Be Painful and Expensive But We've Seen Nothing Yet', *The Independent*, 22 July 2008; independent.co.uk/873652.html (accessed March 2012).

Birkenstock

SICHER BEQUEM

SCHÖN

The church archives from 1774 in the town of Langenberg, north-western Germany, list one Johann Adam Birkenstock as a 'subject and shoemaker'; in 1896 his descendant Konrad Birkenstock opened two speciality shoe shops in the city of Frankfurt am Main, and began to manufacture insoles.

Such were the beginnings of one of the world's best-known and -recognized, not to mention best-loved, shoe brands, now undeniably part of the canon of modern footwear, gaining an iconic status alongside many less practical styles for its comfort, durability and characteristically fashionable pragmatism. Birkenstocks are not univer-sally liked – some say they are an archetypal 'ugly' shoe – but so high is the status of such classic styles as the two-strap Arizona sandal (opposite) and the Boston clog that several luxury fashion powerhouses, from Jil Sander to Marc Jacobs, have created similarly sturdy cork-soled models in a knowing tribute to this most enduring – and divisive – of shoes.

During the First World War, Konrad Birkenstock was granted a contract to prod-uce shoes for German soldiers wounded in

Characterized by a moulded cork sole, Birkenstocks began life in Germany as comfortable shoes that offered health benefits for wounded soldiers. Pictured opposite is the Arizona, the classic two-strap sandal; the bestselling Madrid style is shown below.

The company developed its current, more flexible cork-latex sole in the 1960s. It is contoured with arch support for ease of walking. Pictured above is the Milano sandal.

stability for the back of the foot as it lands on the downward stroke of the walking motion, and the heel cup, which maintains the heel profile and the integrity of a straightened Achilles tendon.

All these trademark aspects come on a sole that is rendered in cork latex, an extremely flexible material that bends with the foot in motion, and lined in suede leather to ensure a healthy temperature and to absorb excess moisture. The Birkenstock principle is that the health of one's feet is crucial to one's more general well-being, a notion that has promoted the success of the brand for more than one hundred years.

By 1925 Birkenstock had acquired a large factory in Friedberg and was exporting his shoes, with their patented 'blue insoles', to Luxembourg, Austria, Sweden, Denmark and Italy, among other countries. The native German market was equally keen on the health-promoting sandals, and by 1932 more than 5000 specialists had begun attending footwear seminars – the famous 'Birkenstock training courses' – in Germany, Austria and Switzerland. Medical experts of the day heartily approved of the 'Birkenstock system', and in 1947 Carl Birkenstock published *The Birkenstock Orthopaedic System*, a book that is still in circulation within the industry more than sixty years later.

action and recuperating in the orthopaedic ward of the nearby Frankfurt–Friedrichsheim hospital. The success of the soles lay in the fact that they were contoured to suit perfectly the foot and the mechanics of walking, from the deep heel cup to the raised arch support and roomy toe box.

Each sole has an elevated footbed edge, designed to protect the toes, and a toe bar, which sits underneath the toes in repose and encourages the natural rolling motion of the foot in action. The cross arch support, a raised section in the middle of the sole that extends from just below the ball of the foot down the inner edge, helps to redirect pressure from the vulnerable middle of the foot to the front. This is compounded by both inner and outer longitudinal arch supports about three-quarters of the way along the sole, towards the heel, to provide

The son of Carl Birkenstock – confusingly, Karl Birkenstock – was the one who led the brand to widespread commercial success during the 1960s, when a vogue for natural products and health awareness gave the company something of a lift. He produced some of the models that went on to become famous:

the Madrid style first appeared in this decade as a 'gymnastic sandal'. He also developed the cork-latex sole, a more flexible alternative to the original cork version, as well as a mechanical moulding machine, which sped up production. In 1982 the brand launched a range of best-selling thong sandals, their success and ubiquity achieved through the mechanization of the production process.

Birkenstocks first arrived in the United States after they were 'discovered' by a tourist, Margot Fraser, on holiday in Germany in 1967. Having found that wearing a pair helped to clear up a back injury, she set up a business to import them exclusively to the States.

Since their first appearance, Birkenstocks have had a firm hold on the market, but the brand's success has a cultural index

quite apart from the health-giving benefits of the shoes themselves. The rise of the hippy in the 1970s meant a boom in sales of Birkenstocks as well as the emergence of a social stereotype of the Birkenstock wearer. During the American presidential election primaries in 2004, several conservatives derided the supporters of candidate Howard Dean as 'Birkenstock liberals'.

The shoes also saw an upturn during the 1990s, when the Austrian designer Helmut Lang paired them with his minimalist urban clothes for his New York catwalk shows. However, when the lead singer of the rock band Jane's Addiction, Perry Farrell, was pelted with a Birkenstock during a concert in Los Angeles in 1990, he commented: 'The guy threw a Birkenstock. I mean, this guy is a real moron: he doesn't even understand fashion.'

Advertisements from Birkenstock's archive illustrate the iconic status of the brand and the company's pride in the calisthenic benefits of its shoes.

Camilla Skovgaard

The Danish shoe designer Camilla Skovgaard (born 1973) has been described by *The Times* as the Arne Jacobsen of couture, and there is an architectural functionalism inherent in many of her pieces that proves the comparison correct. 'I tend to use monasteries, graveyards and elements of Bauhaus as reference points', she says. 'Combining contrasting elements such as fluidity and severity, restraint and sophistication plays an integral part in my design. The emphasis is on form, materials and style, rather than decoration.'[1]

Skovgaard's chosen look tallies with a contemporary mood in fashion for stark, minimalist pieces, but her ergonomic and subtly space-age designs lack none of the drama and dressiness that consumers have come to expect from a statement shoe. 'I make shoes with a fluid, edged line', she says. 'Elegant, with a whiff of barbaric starkness and the subversive.'[2] Skovgaard is one of a clutch of Scandinavian designers who have breached the global fashion market to realign international tastes and trends with Nordic sensibilities. Restraint and equilibrium, clarity of aspect and practicality, undercut with a vision of the gothic, of melancholia and of sombreness rendered in (usually) a monochrome palette – such design heritage is apparent in Skovgaard's work, yet she channels it towards a new type of glamour, a reinvention of the traditionally feminine high heel.

Skovgaard first worked as a couturier to the female members of a sheikh's family in Dubai. After seven years, in 2000, she went to London, where she began training as a shoemaker at Cordwainers, before embarking on a postgraduate course at the prestigious Royal College of Art in 2003. 'When I lived in Dubai, designing couture for the sheikhs' wives and daughters, I noticed that shoes were often an afterthought', she says of her decision to enter a notoriously difficult specialism. 'I read an article about Cordwainers, hid it in my drawer, and when I was ready for the next big step in my career, I applied and attended.'

During her time at Cordwainers, Skovgaard's label began to take off: the American luxury department store Saks Fifth Avenue bought her first collection while she was still studying. In the wake of this early backing, the United States was Skovgaard's biggest market for many years,

Skovgaard's designs are informed by a purist sensibility, with a neo-gothic take on modern monochrome. These are the black-leather 'trashbag' boots from her Pre-Fall collection of 2012.

Right (from left) Ginnifer Goodwin at the premiere of *Something Borrowed* (May 2011); Gwyneth Paltrow at her book signing (April 2011); Dianna Agron at the premiere of *Glee: The 3D Concert Movie* (August 2011)

Below Stilettos from Skovgaard's Pre-Fall collection of 2012.

but Asia and Russia have since caught up, as high-end stockists have bought into her aesthetic. Asian buyers remain the most reliable at purchasing Skovgaard's more challenging designs, such as a pair she developed in 2007, trimmed with human hair. 'Unconventional shapings with architecturally inspired treads are at the fore,' she says of her collections, 'but I don't seem to be able to stay away from hairs and drapes that drag along the floor for more than a season or so.'

Black-leather concealed-platform ankle boots with a spindly spike heel and hyperbolically ridged treads have become Skovgaard's signature, and have developed over time into court shoes and sandals in various shades. But such is the interplay between rigidity and fluidity in her work that even her most sturdy boots have an inherent softness to them, intensified by the sweeping slope of the upper and rounded toe.

In 2010 Skovgaard won British *Elle*'s Accessories Designer of the Year award, and scooped the same gong in her native country. She has since staked her claim on an industry dominated by men making shoes for women, embracing the same technical challenges but adding her own sense of everyday pragmatism. In her collections, one sees the intuitive quest for perfect design, but it is imbued with an interest in function, too. The synthesis of sexy and sturdy is key to the look and feel of Skovgaard's shoes.

'A feeling for and affinity with eroticism, architecture and classicism inspire me to create pieces that adhere not to the standard of a season, but rather to a state of mind or personal style', she explains. Indeed, the footwear she creates nestles implicitly in the bracket with that of such designers as Gareth Pugh and Rick Owens, those riding the wave of a neo-goth zeitgeist, fusing punkish severity and ascetism with grown-up elegance and sophisticated glamour. Such aesthetics do not change much from season to season, and the look has endured, a development of the urban- and clubwear of the 1990s. 'Overall I aim for considered, pared-down detailing', Skovgaard says, 'and intellectual sophistication.'

1. Quoted in Harriet Walker, 'Scandinavian Invasion: How Swedes and Danes Have Stormed the British High Street', *The Independent*, 23 October 2011; independent.co.uk/life-style/fashion/features/Scandinavian-invasion-how-swedes-and-danes-have-stormed-the-british-high-street-2372874.html (accessed February 2012).
2. All quotations from Camilla Skovgaard are taken from email correspondence with the author, January/February 2012.

Architecture and sculptural elements create a romantic feel with a tough edge. Pictured on this page are (clockwise from left) a black wedge sandal from Autumn/Winter 2010–11; a black sandal from Autumn/Winter 2011–12; and a black ankle wedge boot from the 2012 Cruise collection.

Camper

Since its global launch in 1992, the Spanish brand Camper has become synonymous with high quality of design, ecology and the democratization of shopping. Named after the Catalan word for 'peasant' and made in a traditional way, Camper shoes strive to be functional, durable, simple and, above all, comfortable.

Camper traces its lineage back to the late nineteenth-century shoemakers of Majorca, and the industrialization of that trade by Antonio Fluxa, who built the first advanced shoemaking factory on the island in 1877. His grandson Lorenzo founded Camper under that name in 1975, combining the traditional manufacturing methods with a more modern outlook in terms of design and ambition. The name was chosen for its rustic simplicity: Camper's identity is rooted in the Mediterranean – a fact that explains the flashes of wit and irony in its designs – but it is also the identity of those who make the shoes. Each model has practicality and comfort at its heart; informed by the history of their surroundings and by people who live and work outdoors, these shoes are updated for an urban audience only by way of aesthetic additions.

Opposite The Wabi style by Camper, in vulcanized rubber, combines function and futurism, in the flexible and comfortable aesthetic to which the company has always adhered.

Left Camper's shopping bags, like its advertising campaigns and store interiors, have been curated by a number of leading visual and conceptual artists, to enhance the eclectic feel of the brand.

Left, bottom The original nineteenth-century shoemakers on the island of Majorca, where Camper was established in 1877.

Camper's extensive marketing strategies and advertising campaigns celebrate the individualism that remains at the heart of the brand.

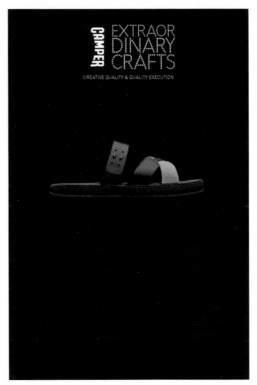

With that in mind, there is an ergonomic feel to Camper shoes. Many are moulded to the foot and appear almost anthropological in their shape, so fitted to the wearer are they. The designs are emphatically sturdy, inspired by the traditional footwear of farm workers, in clog shapes and mule slip-ons, while bright colours and finishes provide a fashionable update for audiences who find rusticism anachronistic. Camper's slogan, 'walk, don't run', subverts the urban code with a more nostalgic pace.

The brand's first shop opened in Barcelona in 1991, heralding widespread interest in what was seen as an organic, homegrown label. It benefitted not only from its Catalan roots, but also from the interest in Barcelona as a cultural hub in the run-up to the Olympic Games held there in 1992. In the Olympic year, in fact, Camper expanded to Paris, London and Milan; today there are stores in more than forty-five countries.

When launching the Barcelona store, executives at the label decided they wanted

Camper was established to cater to the workaday needs of labourers, but styles have become more trend-led and urban, a shift that is particularly apparent in the women's designs.

to revolutionize the way people bought shoes, and chose to make their store more like a fashion boutique than a shoe shop. They presented all the shoes in all sizes, so that customers could rifle through and try them on just as they would a coat or a jumper, without having to collar an employee to find their size. The strategy proved popular with Camper's more left-field clients, who disliked the traditional rigmarole of being fitted for shoes, and it also cut down overheads.

The idea is that each store should have a different layout, feel and concept. In London's Regent Street branch the shoes are attached to the walls with Velcro, while the footwear in Tokyo's Omotesando store is laid out as though it were food at a banquet. Despite the variety, each store must reflect the individual, idiosyncratic Mediterranean flair that informs the brand. Camper's innovative use of retail space anticipated the early twenty-first-century vogue for 'pop-up shops'; with its 'Walk in Progress' initiative it opened temporary structures without the usual fittings of a shop, supplying only the customer's most basic footwear needs: they could try and buy, but they need not expect fancy facades or decorative finishes. Given the brand's reputation for honesty and integrity, the initiative proved as popular as the shoes.

Camper has invested time and effort in developing a marketing strategy that it feels really conveys the language of the brand. In doing so, it has become famous for its graphic, often highly artistic campaigns. Collaborating with a number of well-known artists and designers, such as

Camper is known for the vein of surrealism and humour that runs through its designs.

Right Kremer men's shoe, Spring/Summer 2012.

Right, bottom Camper collaborated with the fashion designer Bernhard Willhelm to create this distinctive hiking trainer for Spring/Summer 2012.

Camper combines a reputation for complex design with the need for comfort and a keen sense of aesthetics.

Fernando Amat, Carlos Rolando and Shiro Miura, Camper has redesigned stores according to the vision of each partner, creating a method of footwear retail that remains unique. So much is obvious in its brand imagery, too, with interpretations of Cubism, archetypal propaganda literature and absurdist humour all present.

As such, Camper has become a brand that customers feel they can trust, no doubt partially because its shoes really are as hard-wearing as they purport to be. There is a special bond between customer and foot-wear brand that does not exist when a customer is buying clothing, and Camper understands and uses it perfectly. We need to be able to trust shoes, and Camper, for all its heartfelt simplicity, has built its reputation on this rather complex notion.

Charles Jourdan

ogether with Manolo Blahnik and Roger Vivier (pp. 99–102 and 145–47), Charles Jourdan is an artisan name that can be credited with inventing fashionable footwear as we know it. Working in the decades before these industry titans came to the fore, he did for shoes what the great couturiers of the era did for clothing, and his is a name that resounds with theirs through the annals of fashion.

Having trained as a shoemaker, Jourdan (1883–1976) opened a shoe shop after returning from the war in 1919, in the town of Romans-sur-Isère in the Drôme, a region of France known for its footwear industry. Two years later he was able to move his premises to the town's main street, boulevard Voltaire, and to employ thirty people; his designs had taken hold of the town's consciousness for their quality and their inimitable sense of style.

In the 1930s Charles Jourdan was the first footwear brand to advertise in high-end fashion magazines and the style press, thereby aligning his name with those of the great Parisian couture houses and bringing in even more business. By 1947 his three sons, René, Charles and Roland, had joined

Charles Jourdan's name resonates through French fashion history, culminating in the modern incarnation of his classic-with-a-twist style. Pictured here are Barbara 1 (opposite; Spring/Summer 2012), a sandal from the Autumn/Winter 2010–11 collection (left) and the interior of the company's Paris boutique (left, bottom).

the label; in 1950 the name, team and business were strong enough to expand beyond France to Britain, where socialites, debutantes and even royals began buying up Jourdan's elegantly heeled designs.

Although the headquarters remained in Romans, a Paris flagship store opened in 1957, and by 1959 Charles Jourdan, along with Roger Vivier, held the licence to create shoes for the Christian Dior couture ranges. In the early years of the following decade, Jourdan also secured the licence to create shoes for Dior's former assistant Pierre Cardin, who was making a name for himself with his feminine and futuristic take on womenswear and couture.

During these years, the Charles Jourdan label was seen as an innovative, inventive force in the fashion industry, rivalled only in its pursuit of new materials by the American designers Herbert and Beth Levine. In the 1960s and '70s the brand secured its fashion and commercial credentials – as well as a place in the history books – by using images taken by the photographer Guy Bourdin for its advertisements. Bourdin's monochrome, smoky, atmospheric settings were at once sensuous and avant-garde, cementing Jourdan's place at the forefront of the fashionable set.

In 1975 the label diversified into handbags and ready-to-wear clothing. Jourdan himself died the following year, but his son Roland continued to run the company. As well as selling the classic Charles Jourdan heeled pump, Roland pioneered new products, including buckled styles that referenced tailoring, and attempted to link the accessories to the label's clothing. When he retired

Jourdan's trademark is femininity, rendered in an *haute bourgeois* vein. Styles on these pages are from Autumn/Winter 2011–12 (opposite and left) and Autumn/Winter 2010–11 (below).

Right The resurrection of the brand in 2010 has meant that Jourdan's legacy lives on in modern footwear design. From top are Pauline 1, Elsa and Ottavia (all Spring/Summer 2012).

Far right Matching shoes and bag by Charles Jourdan, France, 1966.

in 1981, however, the label became more conservative and commercially focused.

Despite a flare-up of bad publicity over the Imelda Marcos scandal – when armed police raided the politician's home in the Philippines in 1986 and discovered more than 2000 pairs of shoes, several by Charles Jourdan among them – the label remained a figurehead of the French couture system. In 1996 it released a perfume called Stiletto to celebrate its seventy-fifth anniversary; the scent came in a bottle in the shape of the Eiffel Tower, in homage to the city that had made the brand great.

In 1999 the Paris flagship store relocated to the Champs-Élysées, but it remained open for less than two years before the firm went bankrupt with debts of $9 million, and sales declined to only 65,000 pairs of shoes per year. The family sold its stake in the business to a Luxembourg-based investment fund, which kept the label open and installed the shoe-designer Patrick Cox as creative director in

Far left Advertising campaign from Autumn/Winter 2011–12.

Left, top and bottom Shoes from Spring/Summer 2011.

2003. In 2005 that role was taken by the Belgian minimalist designer Josephus Thimister, but the Charles Jourdan factories in Romans closed in 2007, marking an end to the company's output.

However, the acquisition of the name (along with that of the classic French designer Stephane Kélian) in 2008 by the Groupe Royer investment fund revitalized the brand under the umbrella of a 'Made in France' initiative. The Autumn/Winter 2010–11 collection saw Ernesto Esposito, who trained under Sergio Rossi in the 1970s and has made footwear for Chloé, Marc Jacobs, Sonia Rykiel and Louis Vuitton, take the reins of this most prestigious of French names. He has brought to it his signature bright, feminine colours in a variety of styles that recall and imitate the original work of the house's founder, but make it relevant for a new and modern audience.

Charlotte Olympia

Although known for her vertiginous heels, the footwear designer Charlotte Olympia Dellal (born 1981) also creates luxurious flat slippers in velvet, and mod-inspired buckle-top brogues in stiff leather. It is this blend of diverse reference points that has made her one of the most delightfully idiosyncratic shoe brands of the twenty-first century so far.

Dellal is the daughter of the Brazilian model Andrea Dellal and the property tycoon Guy, and grand-daughter of the billionaire banker and property investor 'Black' Jack Dellal. She graduated in footwear design from Cordwainers, London, in 2004, and spent time as an intern at the French fashion house Ungaro and couturier Giambattista Valli before setting up her own company in 2007.

Dellal's pieces were an immediate hit among a nascent crowd of east London It-girls, including Alexa Chung and Dellal's own sister, the Mohican-haired model Alice. But Charlotte Olympia is not the vanity project of a designer surrounded by cool friends: it is a label backed by wit and skill, and its astronomic rise is proof of that.

Some of Dellal's most recognizable and famous pieces are those that have cleverly

Opposite Bruce in black, with miniature tiger head.

Left Dolly, in black suede.

Left, bottom Charlotte Olympia Dellal models her own creations. The designer believes that 'the higher the heels, the better you feel!'

Right (from left) Lucy Liu at the premiere of *Erickson Beamon: The Redemption of Eve & Return to the Garden* (September 2011); Alexa Chung at the British Fashion Awards (November 2011); Olivia Palermo at the Jaeger show, London Fashion Week (February 2011).

Below Paloma.

subverted a zeitgeist or chimed with contemporary humour. Velvet smoking slippers in an establishment shade of rich burgundy are decorated with the embroidered features of a cartoon cat – whiskers, ears and all – while a pair of pumps was created in a jigsaw-puzzle effect from lots of pieces of fruit (opposite). These shoes (dubbed the Carmen Miranda), with their charming banana side panels, won particular acclaim during a season in which such designers as Stella McCartney and Miuccia Prada also unveiled designs featuring the contents of their fruit bowls. More recently, Dellal has experimented with fine filigree curlicues of wrought metal used as a mesh to support the weight of the wearer.

'Classic high heels with a modern silhouette in a rainbow of colours and with plenty of leopard print' is Dellal's description of her collections, citing her inspiration as anything from porcelain and Persian rugs to the crime writer Agatha Christie.[1] Her trademark design has to be the Dolly court shoe (p. 37), an updated staple given a 5½-inch (14-cm) heel and what Dellal describes as her 'signature "island" platform', a chunky 2-inch (5-cm) block that sits towards the ball of the foot and adds heft to the front of the shoe, allowing Dellal to experiment with ever higher heels.

This 'island', although a design feature in itself, works almost counter-intuitively to the rest of the shoe. After several years of the concealed platform being at the forefront of footwear trends, Charlotte Olympia's island platforms are conspicuously blocky, often deliberately rendered in a colour and finish different from those of the shoe. The Dolly, for example, comes

Bananas Is My Business,
shoe in python skin,
Spring/Summer 2011.

in everything from grosgrain silk to paisley print, yet the island platform remains a block of plain colour, be it gold, green or red, to add to the graphic nature of Dellal's designs.

Dellal opened a flagship store on Maddox Street in Mayfair, London, in 2010, and was awarded the Accessory Designer prize by the British Fashion Council in 2011. She is one of several young designers in London to experiment with form and function in a brighter, bolder way, leaving the architecture of footwear to her contemporaries, such as Nicholas Kirkwood (pp. 117–21) and Atalanta Weller, but working through the very ergonomics of the shoe. Dellal designs to the extremes of balance and gravity without losing sight of her customers' comfort and ease, not to mention their sartorial inclinations.

Flashes of intense colour and the leopard print she mentions

Right Pandora clutches.

Below Kitty flats.

mark Dellal's demographic with a certain hyper-femininity and even nostalgia. These are brash references worked into something not immediately elegant: Charlotte Olympia shoes are certainly challenging, but customers do not seem to be put off. If anything, Dellal's success is proof of a recent swing towards braver, more directional tastes in footwear. Conservative shoes have fallen out of fashion, in favour of the cartoonish brights of this young designer.

Dellal also invokes the glamour of the 1940s, harking back to a time when the queens of celluloid exuded an almost Amazonian strength. Her platform Mary-Janes and ankle-strapped wedge sandals would not look out of place on the feet of screen legend Lana Turner. Plenty of stars of stage and screen wear her designs, from the actor Sienna Miller to the clothes horse and trendsetter Kate Moss – a sure-fire way for any designer to achieve cult status almost overnight.

But beyond the spotlight and the A-list coterie, Charlotte Olympia remains a label informed by the sort of surrealist humour and aesthetic vision that the designer Elsa Schiaparelli (1890–1973) sought to emulate. 'In difficult times, fashion is always outrageous', she said – and Charlotte Olympia's outrageousness is sublime.

1. Taken from email correspondence between Charlotte Olympia Dellal and the author, December 2011–February 2012.

Surrealism

While some designers experiment with clothing, others expend their most imaginative efforts on shoes. A strong vein of surrealism runs through modern shoe design, as creators have become intent on making footwear ever more fantastic and whimsical. Wit and *trompe l'œil* abound, especially on the most exclusive catwalks.

For Spring/Summer 2006, Alber Elbaz of Lanvin spoke of 'designing shoes like varnished cars – like a Cadillac!',[1] and this was apparent in double-strapped platform sandals with conical heels and uppers that recalled the contrasting colours of those singular bonnets. But Miuccia Prada went one step further for Spring/Summer 2012 (seen above on Katy Perry), showing spindly shoes that referenced the mid-century automobile motifs on the clothing in her collection, shaped from patent leather into plumes of exhaust, and with tail lights on their heels. 'The shoes?' she said backstage. 'The shoes were a joke!'

But we love this sort of witticism: it is proof of a flexibility that does not exist in clothing. Customers feel they can be more daring with shoes, and that has resulted in an array of surrealist styles: Charlotte Olympia's fruit-salad sandals (p. 39), with cut-leather renderings of

apples and bananas, and smoking slippers with embroidered feline faces (opposite); Marc Jacobs's patented 'mouse shoes' either in illustrated patent leather or three-dimensional, with beady eyes and whiskers attached to ponyskin uppers. Jacobs added large furry moustaches to the shoes in his Spring/Summer 2010 collection for Louis Vuitton, and experimented with deconstructed courts for his own label in Spring/Summer 2008, with pumps floating above a horizontal heel that extended from the ball of the foot to counterbalance the wearer.

Throughout the 1930s Elsa Schiaparelli worked with many artists – including the surrealist Salvador Dalí – most notably on a hat made from a shoe worn upside down on the head. In 1984 the Japanese shoemaker Tokio Kumagai presented a collection called Shoes to Eat, which featured brogues made from panelled plastic charcuterie meats. For Spring/Summer 2009 the Swedish designer Ann-Sofie Back showed a clothing collection inspired by the plastic-surgery culture among celebrities, in which spike-heeled stilettos were encased in cling film. And for Autumn/Winter 2012–13, as part of the Central Saint Martins MA group, the graduate designer Anne Thorbjornsen

presented a collection of comically mis-made and uglified pieces; the shoes to match recalled a classic faux pas, with sheets of plastic and toilet paper deliberately stuck to their soles.

But while footwear can be witty in a way that clothing cannot, emboldened by its small scale and unconstrained by codes, surrealism can also take shoes beyond functioning footwear, into the realm of *objets*. Christian Louboutin's collaboration with the film-maker David Lynch in 2007 on a series of portraits involved fetish-style stilettos with heels that protruded far beyond the ball of the foot, never intended to be worn. Similarly, the German designer Iris Schieferstein creates shoes from animal parts, turning horses' hooves into the toecaps of high heels: wearable but distinctly unpalatable.

The champion of the surrealist shoe remains Miuccia Prada, who has also rendered dripping chandeliers as Perspex sandals, spiny stegosaurus crests in ruffles of patent leather, and, most charmingly of all, Mary-Jane heels as a porcelain teacup in her collection for Spring/Summer 2009 for Miu Miu.

1. Quoted in Sarah Mower, 'Lanvin', *Style.com*, 9 October 2005; style.com/fashionshows/review/S2006RTW-LANVIN (accessed May 2012).

Christian Louboutin

I have always thought of women as exotic birds of paradise', says the Parisian designer Christian Louboutin (born 1963). 'I hope that when wearing my shoes, they feel as special as these precious creatures.'[1] Little did he imagine, when he opened his first boutique twenty years ago, that he would teach a generation to appraise shoes in an entirely new way: by their soles.

Louboutin's take on footwear has always been flamboyant, eccentric and exquisite in its unashamed luxury and couture-style finishes. But it was not until two years into trading that Louboutin hit on the red lacquered underside that has made his name and brand a global phenomenon. Inspecting prototypes for a collection in 1993, he was dissatisfied with the contrast between the vibrant upper and the stolid black sole of what would become the best-selling Pensee style. Grabbing a nearby assistant's pot of red nail varnish, so the legend goes, he began to paint the sole crimson. Since then, those glimpses of scarlet (supposedly Pantone 187C, Chinese Red) on red carpets, the front rows of fashion shows and pavements alike have become a sign of quality and fashionable

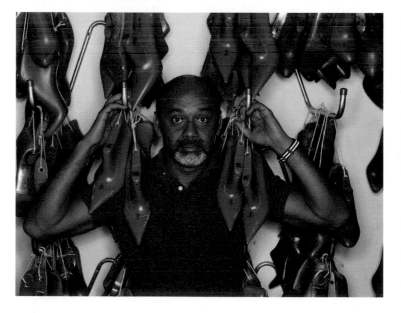

Opposite Sexy 100 court shoe in nude.

Left Athena, Spring/ Summer 2012.

Below, left Christian Louboutin with the lasts in his studio.

Below Carla Bruni-Sarkozy arrives at Zarzuela Palace, Madrid, in April 2009.

Clockwise from right
Piou Piou (Spring/Summer
2012); Janet Dentelle
(Spring/Summer 2012);
Daffodile (Spring/Summer
2012); Lady Daf 160.

status. The idea is also the subject of a court stand-off between Louboutin and the French design house Yves Saint Laurent, which in 2011 stood accused of having copied it; the case rumbles on in New York.

'When I launched the company, I knew nothing about business, only that I wanted to make shoes', Louboutin says. 'I never thought about the future. It's really a lucky star that has brought me to this point, more than ambition, dreams or imagination.'

To celebrate twenty years of the label in 2012, Louboutin released a capsule collection of twenty classic footwear styles and a selection of one-of-a-kind bags (one with a three-dimensional rendering of the Parisian skyline on its shoulder strap). 'Being born and raised in Paris, I have a precise idea of couture and of Parisian elegance', Louboutin adds. A monograph of sketches was published, and the Design Museum in London hosted a retrospective exhibition in Louboutin's honour.

'We wanted to celebrate his career to date', explains the exhibition's curator, Donna Loveday. 'He has built one of the most successful shoe brands in the world, and we want to explain why it has been so successful. These shoes are beautiful things, even divorced from the wearer; you just want to put them in a case and gaze at them.'[2]

Born in 1963 in Paris's 12th arrondissement to a cabinetmaker and a housewife, Louboutin had an unorthodox childhood. He spent as little time at school as he could, and went to live with a friend when

From top Fifi and Loubi Zeppa, both from Spring/Summer 2012.

From top Bambou, Harvanana and Rollerboy Spikes, all Spring/ Summer 2012.

he was twelve. His first job was as an intern at the infamous music hall Les Folies Bergère, where he would help the entertainers backstage. His resulting life-long fascination with cabaret and nightlife shines through in such shoes as La Pluminette and Highness Tina (dedicated to Tina Turner), with Burlesque references and dramatic designs that capture that theatrical glamour for the everyday.

Louboutin's shoes caught the fashionable imagination, with his pioneering innovation of the 'hidden' platform at the ball of the foot, allowing ever higher stilettos. These are seen in his iconic Very Prive and Madame Gres styles, which changed the silhouette of footwear during the 1990s; they are often to be seen on Victoria Beckham, among others. Louboutin shoes are instantly recognizable, even before you contemplate their undersides, for their elegant mix of the sinuous and the architectural.

These are not necessarily shoes in which to go shopping, nor indeed is the wearer expected to be getting in her own groceries. Louboutin does offer some flat shoes (although, notoriously, the lowest heel in his Spring/Summer 2008 collection came in at 5½ inches/14 cm), but the focus is on sexy, spindly height. 'A shoe has so much more to offer than just to walk', he told the *New Yorker* in 2011.[3]

'Wherever possible, I try not to provoke an event', Louboutin says of his creative process. 'Whatever I do always flows from what I've done previously, and my business developed in the same way, without precise goals, with no strategies or projections.' He nevertheless has a wealth of training

From top Echasse, Spring/
Summer 2012; Alfie,
Autumn/Winter 2011–12.

Clockwise from right Creve Coeur, Sex and Disconoeud, all Spring/Summer 2012.

behind him, having worked in his early years for Charles Jourdan, one of the first footwear licensees for Dior in the 1950s, and Roger Vivier, who made Queen Elizabeth II's shoes for her coronation. Parisian club kid Christian Louboutin has grown up to be quite their equal.

1. All quotations from Christian Louboutin are taken from email correspondence with the author, December 2011–February 2012, unless otherwise stated.
2. From telephone conversation between Donna Loveday and the author, March 2012.
3. Quoted in Lauren Collins, 'Soul Mate: Christian Louboutin and the Psychology of Shoes', *New Yorker*, 28 March 2011; newyorker.com/reporting/2011/03/28/110328fa_fact_collins (accessed March 2012).

Collectors

One of the most striking aspects of latterday footwear culture is the tendency to treat shoes as objects and collectables. With the rise in prominence of certain brands has come an increase in the number of people for whom simply acquiring pieces by these names is of greater importance than their use. Shoes have become *objets*, things of great beauty, as manufacturing techniques and tastes have become more complex, and so the number of people buying shoes for a private collection has risen. In the public realm, the Victoria and Albert Museum in London alone has more than 1000 items in its footwear collection.

One of the most notorious collectors of shoes is Imelda Marcos, a Filipina politician and the widow of the tenth president of the Philippines, Ferdinand Marcos. In 1986 she was discovered to own more than 2700 pairs of shoes when she and her husband were forced into exile after a coup. Her shoes – among them designs by Salvatore Ferragamo, Givenchy, Chanel and Christian Dior, all in a size eight and a half – were discovered in a presidential palace (above) and became symbolic of the regime's extravagance in the face of national poverty.

Marcos's successor as president, Corazon Aquino, ordered many of the shoes to be displayed as symbols of corruption and inequality, and in 2001 Imelda (by then re-established as a politician in her own country) was present at the opening of a museum dedicated to shoes, including many from her collection, in Marikina, the heart of the Filipino footwear industry.

In 2010 the designer Christian Louboutin (pp. 43–48) revealed that one of his best customers was the American novelist Danielle Steel, who would often visit his showroom in Paris and leave with as many as eighty pairs. Steel's personal collection is estimated to contain about 6000 pairs of shoes, most of them Louboutins, and to be worth almost £2 million.

Despite having her own eponymous brand of shoes, the actress and singer Jennifer Lopez is also rumoured to be a collector of Louboutin's work, with an estimated 400 pairs. In homage to the brand, she recorded a single called 'Louboutins' (2009), which she performed on the US television show *So You Think You Can Dance*, arriving on stage in a giant mock-up of a red lacquer-soled stiletto. 'I'm throwing on my Louboutins', goes the chorus. 'Watch these red bottoms,/ And the back of my jeans./ Watch me go, bye baby.'

Such is the status of shoe-buying in the twenty-first century that many ordinary women also admit to collecting innumerable pairs. In 2011 a survey by MSN found that the average woman owned thirty-nine pairs of shoes, with more than a quarter admitting to owning more than fifty pairs.[1] Some 47 per cent said they bought a new pair of shoes every month; a further 15 per cent said they invested in footwear every fortnight. With buyers in such numbers as these, it is no surprise that shoes have become a cultural touchstone, and why they seem to many to be the most accessible face of modern fashion.

1. 'Shoe Survey', *MSN Life and Style*, 2 September 2011; style.uk.msn.com/fashion/shoe-survey-the-results-are-in (accessed May 2012).

Church's

Stone Church was a cordwainer, born in 1675, who plied his trade in Northampton and passed his skills on to his family. In 1873 his great-grandson Thomas Church opened a small factory in the town (which has had a reputation for shoemaking since the time of Oliver Cromwell and the seventeenth-century Commonwealth), transforming the wares of the wooden workbench within a few years from local artisan pieces to a rigorously made, high-quality range that was in demand throughout the country and much of Europe.

By the 1880s, then manager William Church was spending most of his time travelling the country to keep on top of orders and enquiries, such was the demand for the company's 'adaptable' shoes. Up to this point, shoemakers had not differentiated between the left and the right foot, creating identical shoes to be worn in on each. But Church & Co. created mirror-image models shaped according to each foot, available in six different widths and a range of materials, and also made in half-sizes. In 1884 the design won the Gold Medal at the International Exhibition at the Crystal Palace, London.

The year 1907 saw the emergence of a market in America, and that has substantially grown as the company's profile has been raised over the past century. In 1921 the company's first London shop opened, selling ladies' 'archmoulded' styles. Women's taste in shoes had become substantially more complex, not only with the developments in fashion that meant that shoes were now prominent and visible beneath shorter hems, but also with the relaxation of social codes that saw women become more active, more physically engaged and more aware of the health benefits of walking. In 1929 a Church's store opened on Madison Avenue in Manhattan; it did not escape the economic rigours of the Depression, but can still be found in the same premises today.

The period between the two world wars saw Church's become actively involved in the evolution of the British footwear industry, co-founding the British Shoe and Allied Trades Research Association in 1919, and partnering with Northampton Technical College (now the University of Northampton) in 1925. Trade during the Second World War focused the brand on

Now owned by the Prada group, Church's makes shoes that speak of quintessentially English taste. The Shanghai shoe of 1929 is pictured opposite (and its modern version shown overleaf).

providing footwear for the armed services, withdrawing from the children's market and developing more women's lines after the conflict ended. The 1950s saw Church's enter the domestic market more fully, with concessions in branches of Austin Reed and through the acquisition of three other British manufacturers, whose resources went towards Church's output. In 1957 a new factory was opened on St James Road in Northampton, where the headquarters of the company still stands. The royal seal of approval was given to the company after a visit in 1965 by the Queen and the Duke of Edinburgh, an avowed wearer of the firm's classic brogues.

There followed a period during which fashions in men's formal shoes did not change much, as tastes for workwear remained similar over about twenty or thirty years. Certainly the stiff, polished leather and stitching of a Church's brogue or winklepicker were known to be hallmarks of a good-quality shoe, and the brand suffered no loss, but the leaps and bounds with which it had progressed so far slowed to a more practical constant.

It was not until the company was bought in 1999 by the Prada group that the brand came to the fore again. In a deal endorsed by the Church family and with the intention of retaining the brand's British identity, the Italian luxury powerhouse – itself with a background in leather goods – brought more credibility and a new audience to the traditional styles that had seen something of a lag in sales.

The 'It' status of the Prada label at that time ensured publicity, while the style set who adored the Italian label moved with equal pleasure to rediscover this domestic name. A taste for androgyny fuelled by subsequent trends for pieces with a vintage sensibility, and most recently by a return to natively manufactured goods, has ensured the survival of the brand and a boost in profile that it could have only dreamed of ten years earlier.

Branches have opened in Paris, Rome and St Moritz, and are planned for Leeds, Edinburgh and Hong Kong. The shoes are still made in Northampton, and take – as they always have – up to eight weeks to be finished, with more than 250 manual stages of assembly. The key part of the Church's manufacturing process is that the sole and upper are stitched to a 'welt' of hand-cut leather before being attached to the bottom of the shoe, so that re-soling can be carried out more efficiently and without damaging the original features of the shoe.

Still resolutely producing the style for which it was first loved, along with the fittings and range of choice that bolstered its reputation, Church's has also branched out into rather more directional models. Alongside the tan leather and black punched brogues, one can find studded variants, or those in white leather, or red with cut-out panels, or even yellow and green, all based on a shoe that has barely changed since its introduction to the market in the mid-nineteenth century.

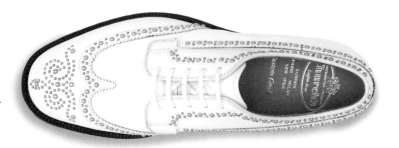

Church's is known for the use of fine-quality leather in traditional styles, but it has broadened its range in recent years, gaining a new and spirited fashionability. The modern version of Shanghai is shown opposite; on this page are shoes from the Spring/Summer 2012 collection, for men (top two styles) and women (bottom two styles).

Clarks

Seen now on the feet of everyone from pensioners and yummy mummies to mods and Britpoppers, the footwear brand Clarks was established by two Quaker brothers in the early nineteenth century. James and Cyrus Clark realized that the offcuts of sheepskin from the Somerset tannery at which they worked could be made into cosy slippers, and these shoes soon became a must-have in the local area. The Brown Petersburg sheepskin-lined slipper, invented in 1825, was selling an average of 1000 pairs a month by 1842, and was commercially so successful that the brothers won two awards at the Great Exhibition at the Crystal Palace in 1851.

What began as a cottage industry became a community endeavour: a network of workers collected the offcuts and other materials, took them home, shaped them and stitched them together to create the finished slipper. Each Friday they would return with the pairs they had made, and collect their wages.

The recession of 1863 hit C. & J. Clark Limited badly, however, and the brothers were forced to consult their Quaker community and ask for a loan to preserve their

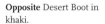

Opposite Desert Boot in khaki.

Left Desert Trek boot.

Below Originals Desert Boots.

Bottom Crafter Cool.

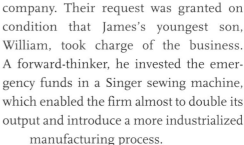

From top Wallabee in black suede; Desert Boot in blush-pink suede; Mask Step.

company. Their request was granted on condition that James's youngest son, William, took charge of the business. A forward-thinker, he invested the emergency funds in a Singer sewing machine, which enabled the firm almost to double its output and introduce a more industrialized manufacturing process.

With that came more products. Launched in 1883, the Hygiene model became the first shoe to be fitted precisely to the wearer's foot, something the brand insists on and for which it has specific methodology even now. But the Clarks did not forget their Quaker roots as the company grew, and the business was as much family-run as it was involved in the community and with the welfare of workers. As innovation increased, too, inexpensive alternatives to silk and satin made a broader variety of fabrics available to a nation increasingly interested in fashion.

As attitudes to formality and leisure altered, and women became more active, the demand for footwear increased. John, Roger and Alice Clark ran the company in the early twentieth century, as hemlines rose infinitesimally and new styles of shoes and boots were sought to show off and support the increasingly visible female ankle.

A children's range was launched in the early 1900s, and the signature Clarks foot gauge became a benchmark in the industry, encouraging care in the fitting of growing feet. The company's first press advertisements came out in the 1930s, leading to a nationwide

rise in sales. Meanwhile, it amalgamated with the footwear brand Peter Lord, which gave it shops across the country, and which would remain a presence on the high street until the mid-1990s. During the Second World War the Clarks factories were used to make torpedoes, but the company persisted, developing a hinged wooden sole to allow the production of shoes to continue despite the shortage of leather.

The post-war years, under the guidance of Bancroft Clark, were busy ones for the brand. The Regent Street flagship store opened in 1957, as well as fifteen new factories up and down the country – the Quaker workforce of Street in Somerset having been overwhelmed by orders and by the popularity of the products. This era also saw a boom in creativity at the company, with the iconic Desert Boot (designed by Nathan Clark) making its first appearance in 1950, and innovations in materials and fabric opening up new possibilities in terms of the development of products.

In the 1990s Clarks had to fall into step with the times and was forced to move production overseas to Portugal. Its factories in the United Kingdom were closed, but the brand continues to be one of the most successful British names in manufacturing. Its classic styles and organic feel were given something of a boost in the mid- to late 1990s, when music stars of the Britpop era, including Liam and Noel Gallagher of Oasis and Richard Ashcroft of the Verve, popularized the label's Desert Boot and simple suede shoes.

Clarks capitalized on this publicity, which culminated in a pair of its Wallabee shoes (opposite, top; first launched by

From top Crafter Boot; Quay Point; Manor Park.

Clockwise from right
Kitzi Bluff; Yarra Bee in
walnut suede; Yarra Desert
in khaki suede.

Lance Clark in 1965) being worn rather conspicuously on the cover of the Verve's best-selling album *Urban Hymns* in 1997, with several successful advertising campaigns. One, with the tagline 'Act your age, not your shoe size', even coined a phrase that has been assimilated into the vernacular.

These most iconic of designs – the Wallabee, the Desert Boot (p. 54) and the Desert Trek (p. 55, top left) – are now part of the Clarks Originals range. This is not a seasonal collection but instead offers timeless products for each generation to discover anew. There may be dips and peaks in popularity, but these styles have proved their longevity. Most recently, the Desert Boot has been worn by singer Florence Welch of Florence and the Machine in an updated version with a low wedge heel, and has since become a strong seller in Japan.

forefront of the mainstream far more often than do their clothing counterparts.

The resurgence of the brothel creeper is a case in point. Originally the shoe of choice for Teddy boys, this stacked lace-up earned its name for the rubber sole, which allowed reprobates to leave late-night lock-ins quietly. More recently, brothel creepers have been used as styling aids on the catwalks of high-end designers, notably those who work in a streetwear vein, such as Emma Cook, and have been picked up by such labels as Chanel and Prada, which gave espadrilles a flatform makeover for Spring/Summer 2011. The brand Underground has become notorious during this revival for its Wulfrun model, a nostalgic update of the Teddy boy creeper, rendered as a black suede lace-up (above) as well as a monochrome loafer.

The extension of the thick sole to the mainstream has brought the footwear of other subcultures into the fashionable spotlight. The sort of heavily embellished metal-finished

the feet of a trend-focused demographic, rather than those of adherents to a music and lifestyle subculture. The high platform trainers of 1990s club culture, made by the German label Buffalo, have also seen a resurgence in sales, and are once more stocked by high-street retailers. Similarly divergent footwear trends also arose in the 1980s and early '90s as a reaction to the more prevalent bourgeois tastes of the day. The emphasis with all these anti-trend looks is on confounding elegance and moving away from the traditional daintiness or smartness that footwear is supposed to provide.

When the Japanese designers Yohji Yamamoto and Rei Kawakubo of Comme des Garçons began showing their avant-garde collections in Paris in 1982, they dressed their models in beaten-up men's brogues, not wishing the accessories to upstage the clothes. As it was, this type of shoe became a byword for sophistication achieved in a more cerebral and challenging way than that offered at the time by mainstream footwear styles. Yamamoto went

Ann Demeulemeester also made their mark on footwear, with Demeulemeester's tough biker boots and Victoriana-style lace-ups becoming something of a calling card and featuring in her collections to this day. Margiela, meanwhile, focused his wit and charm on creating a piece of footwear as subversively playful as his clothing. His Tabi boot, inspired by the traditional split-toe shoes worn by practitioners of martial arts, is now something of a cult item in the wardrobes of the fashionable cognoscenti. Originally made from supple black leather, the boots are now available in oxblood, brown and even gold, with idiosyncratic rounded heels in either opaque plastic or clear Perspex.

Converse

That the brand Converse is more than 100 years old does not perhaps come as much of a surprise given the ubiquity of its name, but it is telling that the broad design of the company's shoes has changed little, giving Converse trainers an almost singular hold on the phrase 'cult classics'.

In February 1908 Marquis Mills Converse, then a respected worker at managerial level in another footwear company, opened the Converse Rubber Shoe Company in Massachusetts. It specialized in winter footwear, in particular sturdy rubber-soled boots for men, women and children to wear in the state's deep snow. By 1910 Converse was producing 4000 pairs of shoes a day.

The transformation from success to phenomenon came in 1915, when the company began using its expertise with rubber soles to produce shoes suitable for playing tennis, a game that was opening up democratically and demographically as class and gender barriers became less rigid. By 1917 Converse had also begun to manufacture basketball shoes – the rubber-soled canvas hi-tops for which it has

Converse is a brand that uniquely managed the crossover from sports to street – and back again.

become so well known – and in 1921, when the basketball player Chuck Taylor came to the factory to complain about having sore feet, he was signed on the spot as a brand ambassador and salesman, a job he kept until his death in 1969.

Taylor's signature was added to the brand's basketball shoes as a design motif in 1923. At that time, Converse also worked on a customized range of basketball shoes for the New York Renaissance (known as the Rens), the first American team to be made up solely of African American players. As was the case for many American manufacturers, the country's entrance into the Second World War in 1941 meant a shift in focus, and during the war years Converse turned its attention to rubberized footwear and clothing for military personnel.

Nevertheless, after the war Converse gained a monopoly among young people, during the golden age of the 'preppy' look, fitting them out for athletics and games at school and, in the nascent years of the 'Youthquake' of the 1960s, giving them a casual alternative to more formal footwear. It also produced the 'Converse Yearbook', one of the first marketing tools of its kind, featuring cover art that reminded students of the vital role the company had played in their high-school days. Throughout the 1950s, '60s and '70s Converse was seen as an iconic brand – the only option for sports footwear – and in the 1970s the company bought the rights to the Jack Purcell shoe, creating yet another cult trainer.

Subsequent years, however, brought a sportswear revolution, with the emergence

of such specialist brands as Puma, Adidas, Nike and, later, Reebok. These names introduced more design-heavy, trend-led models to the market, and Converse suddenly seemed to be the shoe of yesteryear, even losing the title of Official Shoe of the National Basketball Association.

Business continued, buoyed slightly by the adoption by many grunge musicians in the 1990s of Converse hi-tops as their footwear of choice, but the company was forced to file for bankruptcy in 2001. It was bought by the conglomerate Footwear Acquisitions, which drove Converse's stake in the market up from sixteenth to eighth; executives at Nike then took note and bought the company in 2003 for $305 million.

Since then Converse has cemented its place in the market, not necessarily as a sports shoe any more, but as a streetwear trainer, conspicuous on pavements and in magazines alike. It has a specific indie-musician following, something on which it capitalized in 2006 when it brought in the designer John Varvatos to create a clothing line.

The Converse range still includes the Chuck Taylor All Star basketball shoe, now in a plethora of colours and recently modified for a slimmer fit and less chunky sole; it comes in the original hi-top model, as well as a low-cut and even a knee-high version. The re-release of the Weapon hi-top trainer of 1986, emblazoned with the star

Opposite, top All Star hi-tops with American fabric.

Opposite, bottom left American football stars Milt Plum, Jim Brown and Bobby Mitchell, Cleveland, Ohio, 1959.

Opposite, bottom right Basketball player Wilt 'The Stilt' Chamberlain, 1948.

Left All Star hi-top.

Below Converse X Undefeated Born Not Made.

Bottom Converse All Star trainers collection.

Right Rihanna, September 2005; Russell Brand at the British Comedy Awards, May 2009.

Below White All Star trainers.

and chevron motif designed by Converse employee Jim Labadini in the 1970s, has also had some success, even spawning two evolutionary styles: the Loaded Weapon (2003) and the Weapon EVO (2009).

Collaborations and special editions have also proved popular with Converse customers, who classically refer to them as 'Cons' or 'Chucker boots'. In recent years there have been updates to the Chuck Taylor by stars and characters as diverse as Metallica, the Ramones, the Clash, DC Comics and Dr Seuss, and even high-heeled versions were briefly available.

Converse still sponsors college basketball teams in the States, including the Western Kentucky Hilltoppers, and a number of professional basketball players still wear Converse designs, among them Kyle Korver, Elton Brand and J.J. Barea, as well as 'Big Baby' Glen Davis.

Trainer Freaks

The 1980s gave birth to many things, among them hip hop and wealth culture. And it was the confluence of these two that produced the new phenomenon of 'Sneakerheads', diehard trainer obsessives whose lives revolved around collecting limited editions, rare makes and vintage classics. A collection of training shoes designed in 1985 by the basketball player Michael Jordan for the athletics brand Nike – Air Jordan – sold out so quickly that fans were forced to go to great lengths to get their hands on a pair, and subsequent collections from other brands, such as Reebok and Adidas, played on the scarcity that had formed this culture for increasing sales.

The phenomenon has also had an impact on the development of trainers and the evolution of taste. Sneakerheads prefer limited editions with identifying characteristics; therefore, brands have used collaborations with artists, one-off colourways and in-store customization techniques, such as Nike ID, to create shoes that will become collectors' items. Some of the most successful initiatives have been celebrity endorsements, including those by the rappers Missy Elliott and Run-DMC (above, right), whose versions of the thirty-five-year-old Adidas Superstar style in 2006 sold

out. More recently, the musician Kanye West created Air Yeezy for Nike, a style that launched in 2009 and also became a collectors' item.

It is of particular interest that the impetus behind this subculture is not primarily fashion or aesthetics, but the importance of acquisition and street status according to the ethic of hip hop culture. Complexity of design, shape, finish or silhouette have little to do with these essentials.

Since the emergence of the Sneakerhead tribe, which is linked to such activities as skateboarding and break-dancing, brands have offered more and more trainers, in more varied designs; those for women have particularly increased. The movement has also affected trends and taste in the fashion side of the business, with a resurgence of enthusiasm for nostalgic hi-top styles, as these are the ones in which serious Sneakerheads are more interested.

The advent of the Sneakerheads has also led to a rash of collaborations between designers and sportswear brands to produce signature trainers. The avant-garde, cartoonish designer Jeremy Scott has worked with Adidas on a streetwear range that has so far included hi-tops embellished with silver wings, in the manner of classical deities, and a pair that featured stuffed artificial panda and tiger heads

attached to the Velcro fastenings. Each has sold out, especially after endorsement from celebrities on television and in magazines. Giles Deacon designed a pair of Converse in support of the Project Red AIDS charity.

'Sneakerology', as it is known, has necessitated a new language in sportswear, one that goes beyond practicality and fit; several stores now cater only for those seeking rare and vintage styles, and counterfeiting has become more of a problem. In 2011 the chain Foot Locker launched 'Sneakerpedia.com', a wiki-based online community for collectors, and Carnegie Mellon University, Pennsylvania, offers a social history course called 'Sneakerology 101'.

Gil Carvalho

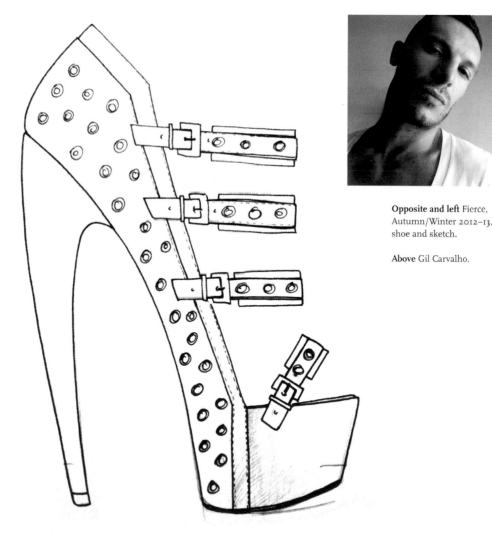

When Gil Carvalho launched his first own-brand collection in 2003, it was the era of the uber-shoe: that is to say, the shoe that not only pushed the boundaries of product design in terms of concept and embellishment, but also exerted distinct pressure on the wearer, in its height, shape and centre of gravity. His designs fitted perfectly into the school of maximalist, architectural footwear that was coming to the fore. These statement shoes took not a little inspiration from a fetishistic subculture, subsuming sexual peccadilloes into the mainstream and recasting them according to fashionable taste. 'I like creating objects of desire', Carvalho says. 'Sculptural shoes that are designed to empower women. Sharp, sleek and sexy.'[1]

Having studied fine art and history in his native Portugal, Carvalho came to London to continue as a student of architecture. That discipline is obvious in his highly constructed but delicately wrought pieces, in which slashed, latticed, webbed and punched leather creates fluid and permeable uppers with an impression of solidity, even toughness.

Opposite and left Fierce, Autumn/Winter 2012–13, shoe and sketch.

Above Gil Carvalho.

At first characterized by exaggerated platforms and insteps swooping to slim and tapering heels, Carvalho's shoes have become sturdier during his career; none of the bulk has been taken from the front, but thicker heels create an armoured effect from behind. Some of these curve inwards, part-banana or comma heel, in Carvalho the architect's constant search for the perfectly cantilevered angle, and any weight on the sole is offset by delicate – sometimes non-existent – uppers, made minimal with open-faced buckles or thin plaited strips of leather. Carvalho likes to open up the foot; his is not the stompy, clompy aesthetic often associated with such extreme platforms. 'The main aim is to achieve a cohesive selection of styles that will appeal to the customer in various ways', he explains of the breadth of his collections, which often span the gamut of shoe types, from boots to sandals, in the same season: 'from a more casual or practical look, to the most sophisticated and intricate designs, without compromising on essence and style'.

After obtaining his degree in shoe design from Cordwainers in London, Carvalho began an internship at Vivienne Westwood, a label noted for its innovation in footwear as well as its tendency towards hyperbole in this discipline (witness the Super Elevated Gillie style, a 9-inch/22.8-cm platform brogue, which brought down the supermodel Naomi Campbell at a catwalk show in 1993, or the iconic Rocking Horse Sandal, which offered as much stability as its name implies). He went on to set up shop in his own name, and in 2006 Carvalho became one of the first high-end footwear brands to collaborate with a high-street store, when

Clockwise from far left
Buzz; silver shoe from
ready-to-wear collection;
Brave; Etoile.

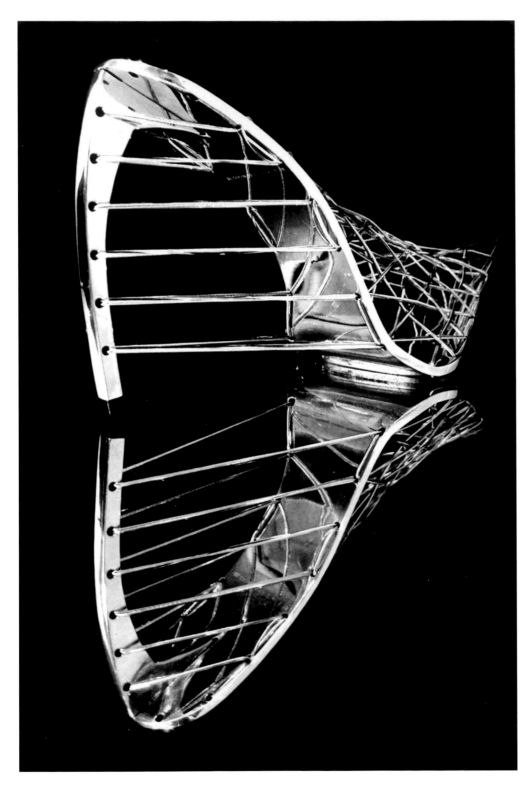

he designed a diffusion range for the footwear chain Faith. These shoes were commercially minded, and therefore less exaggerated than his mainline designs, but among them were three styles that really encapsulated the tastes of the time through elevated platforms, metallic finishes and higher heels than usually seen on the high street. They were part of a sea-change in footwear trends, as the concealed platform, championed by such high-end designers as Carvalho and Christian Louboutin (see pp. 43–48), became more widely available and accessible to those on a budget.

'There's always an architectural feel to my work that I like to enhance through details and textures,' Carvalho says, 'a combination of style, high heels and the slashed leather effect that I've developed and used throughout my collections. Styles such as Ivy or Buzz are perfect examples that combine all these elements. Each collection is like a small family and each style is somehow linked ... following the theme of the collection. I have created a strong bond with architecture, from my previous studies, and it remains a constant reference and source of inspiration.'

So much is clear from the almost Bauhaus lines of many of Carvalho's designs; caged shoe-boots and an exploration of linear structure pick up on many design quirks of the Art Deco era, too. Soft and subtle metallics, such as brushed bronze and platinum leather, recall the age of opulence, but stylistic restraint keeps the pieces modern. The use of suede and metal details, such as buckles and rivets, also adds a contemporary hard edge to the aesthetic.

Carvalho aims with each pair to provide 'beauty, empowerment and comfort', and his designs state this in order: they are wondrous, often mind-boggling, to behold; their sturdiness, height and ferocity speak of power and strength; and their structure, carefully considered with the professional eye of an architect, is geared towards practicality and ease. In this way, Gil Carvalho, with his blend of aesthetics and logistics, is a truly modern shoemaker.

1. All quotations from Gil Carvalho are taken from email correspondence with the author, 2012.

Opposite Image from conceptual collection.

Left (left to right) Madonna walking to a party, New York, October 2005; Dannii Minogue, *Cosmopolitan* Ultimate Woman of the Year Awards, London, November 2008; Liz Hurley at the launch of her reality television show *Project Catwalk*, London, December 2005.

Below (left to right) Moët; Comet.

Gina

I n 1954 the Turkish designer Mehmet Kurdash (1924–2010) launched the footwear brand Gina from a basement in Shoreditch, east London. Named after the Italian actress Gina Lollobrigida, the label had one clear directive: to create exquisitely glamorous handmade shoes.

Having since celebrated its fiftieth anniversary, Gina is now run by Kurdash's three grandsons, Attila, Aydin and Altan, and has shod such stars as Nicole Kidman, Penelope Cruz and Melanie Griffith. The brand also supplied shoes for Madonna's Confessions tour in 2006.

'The Gina woman transcends the mere vagaries of seasonal fashion', explains Aydin Kurdash, 'and is characterized by her passionate pursuit of timeless style and elegance, predicated on flawless luxury and never settling for second best.'[1] As such, Gina shoes have a reputation for evoking the glitz and glamour of yesteryear, rarely caving in to trends for structuralism or ascetism. For that, they enjoy huge success. They are unashamedly pretty shoes, of the sort young girls hope one day to own and real-life princesses stop off on Old Bond Street to buy. Heels are tapering, thin

Audrey (opposite) and Beyonce.

stilettos; flats are bejewelled and decorative; the mule is a model that abides in successive collections; hyper-embellishment and strappiness are a signature. According to Aydin, 'superior materials, an expert, handcrafted finish and captivating designs form the basis of [the Gina woman's] shoe wardrobe: the very hallmarks of

the Gina philosophy and our highly esteemed collections.'

It is hardly surprising that there is something of near-Eastern glamour to Gina's blinged-up vibrancy, given the founder's Turkish roots. These heavily encrusted shoes are often to be seen poking out from beneath an abaya, since the boutique has become a destination of note on the retail tourist track for wealthy Arab magnates and their wives spending time in London. Yet there is something of the golden age of Hollywood to the firm's designs, too, and the designers cite the iconic glamour of cinema as their prime reference – fittingly, considering the roots of the brand's name. A delicate and feminine 1950s sensibility can be seen in strappy sandals decorated with rhinestones, and in closed, pointed-toe stiletto Mary-Janes, recalling the wardrobe of a mid-twentieth-century Laurel Canyon costumier, working perhaps on a Cecil B. DeMille motion picture. This is something on which Gina as a brand prides itself: although collections are released seasonally, there is little variation according to trend. The collections serve to highlight new ideas or techniques that the master shoemakers have acquired, rather than catering more broadly to changing tastes. With that in mind, instead of having to search wistfully for a pair that existed for one six-month retail window only, the Gina customer will find favourite models re-released in new colourways each season.

'The Gina woman remains at the very forefront of fashion by

Gina's advertising campaigns are unshamedly opulent, just like the shoes themselves.

eschewing the frivolity of fashion', says Aydin. 'Therein is [her] confident and bold style.' This is indeed a bold statement, given the year-round nature of the industry, focusing no longer on two collections each year, but also on interstitial 'pre-collections' shown as 'resort' and 'cruise'. These ensure that every possible whim is catered to, whatever the climate, as well as offering customers something new to choose from – in this, the internet age of shopping – every two or three months. By opting out of this system, Gina has confidently allied itself with something more like a couture tradition, creating shoes that may not be bespoke, but which are assimilated more easily into the customer's lifestyle simply by being a constant.

'Gina footwear has been gracing the feet of supermodels and leading actresses, as well as high-society celebrities, royal families and an ever-growing following of international stars, for more than fifty years', says Aydin. 'These are discerning women who have no need or desire ever to settle for less than the very, very best.' There have been some concessions to fashion, however, with the introduction of the covered platform so popular during the mid-2000s and the release in 2012 of a Union Jack range, which featured the recognizable cross and colours picked out in crystals on oyster silk platform stilettos. On one pair of flat sandals, four bisecting blue straps re-created the flag on top of the wearer's foot, in a nod to the patriotism of the brand during the Olympic year of its home city.

1. All quotations from Aydin Kurdash are taken from email correspondence with the author, 2011.

From top Elle; Geneva; Loren.

Giuseppe Zanotti

F ashion editors and A-listers alike love the Italian designer Giuseppe Zanotti for having remixed Hollywood glamour with his teetering, spindly high heels in a luscious palette of colours and a daring variety of frilled and fronded cuts. He is a true craftsman, sketching each pair by hand and overseeing its production through to the very final stages.

'He's amazing at what he does', says the supermodel Anja Rubik, who has worked with Zanotti on his advertising campaigns since she first became a model. 'He has so much passion for it – all the time he explores it, and collaborates with other designers. At the end of the day, I'm a woman who likes clothes, bags and jewellery, so working with him is a lot of fun for me, his shoes give me energy – he's a genius, a shoe genius.'[1]

Hailing from a small town near Rimini, in the heart of Italy's footwear region, Zanotti (born 1957) spent his formative years as a DJ in that city's boisterous clubs and on the nightlife circuit before an interest in art and design led him to follow the happenings of the catwalks in Milan and Paris with almost religious fervour. He gave up his career in

Opposite Red, yellow and blue court shoe, 2003.

Above, left Giuseppe Zanotti in his workshop.

Above Swarovski crystal-encrusted heels with dollar-sign motif.

Right Red court shoe, 2003.

Below Pearl-encrusted
sandals designed
by Kanye West.

music to focus on fashion, and began his time as a craftsman working alone and freelance for various firms and design houses. In the early 1990s he decided to move ahead on his own and bought the failing Vicini shoe factory in the Marche region. From that beginning he has built a shoe empire, with his eponymous ultra-luxe label at its heart and several other lines around it. The Vicini company also produces shoes for Balmain, Thakoon, Proenza Schouler and Christopher Kane, all with the 100 per cent guarantee of a 'Made in Italy' mark of origin.

Zanotti, meanwhile, brought to the small factory his own interpretation of the modern artisanal production process. He instigated new and separate departments for jewels and embellishment, a team for the embroidery of shoes and an entire wing to focus on heels. He saw luxury shoes as akin to clothing – and clothing of haute couture levels at that – and resolved that his shoes would not be mass-produced replicas or reissued, once-trendy 'greatest hits'.

Zanotti's first collection was presented in New York in 1994 to great acclaim: his feminine, considered aesthetic, which concentrated on comfort as well as on fashionable finishes, was almost unique in the market. Hard-edged stiletto heels were softened with trimmings of chiffon or layers of silk, while razor-sharp ankle boots and peep-toes in black and patent leathers were as sexy as they were sturdy. A business that began with Zanotti himself and a handful of others soon grew to more than 300 employees. The first standalone boutique opened in Milan in 2000, and was immediately followed by outposts in New York, Paris, London, Moscow and Dubai. Zanotti is known for his involvement at every stage, from the design process to attending trunk shows with customers, even contacting store buyers personally to ensure that they are happy with the deliveries.

Zanotti describes his style as 'naïf and rock'n'roll',[2] as suggested by the many contrasts inherent in his collections, his strict silhouettes and delicate detailing, and his incredible attention to conspicuous and obvious, even opulent, quality in a market that has become more interested in a stealthier sort of luxury. Zanotti's shoes are beacons of complex design and considered creation.

Zanotti also has a reputation within the industry for supporting young designers, who benefit from his expertise and his production outlets. He has worked with several well-known and highly regarded photographers on his campaigns, including the avant-garde Dutch duo Inez van Lamsweerde and Vinoodh Matadin, and is known for his keen interest in research and development.

Giuseppe Zanotti has said that his shoes are intended not to cover the feet but to adorn them and to reference the world around the woman who wears them. In their fluid and sinuous lines, his shoes are inevitably beautiful whenever and however they are worn.

Left Fur-topped boot, 2003.

Below Zanotti has made shoes for a variety of catwalk shows, including those of Victoria's Secret, a lingerie label known for its dramatic, flamboyant presentations.

1. Quoted in 'Fashion Expert Interviews', promotional video; giuseppezanottidesign.com/experience/zanotti/en/giuseppe_zanotti/FashionExpertInterviews.asp (accessed May 2012).
2. Quoted in 'Giuseppe's Story', giuseppezanottidesign.com/experience/zanotti/en/giuseppe_zanotti/story.asp (accessed May 2012).

Havaianas

The flip-flops made by Havaianas were inspired by the Japanese *zori*, a traditional sandal.

Brazilian beach culture gave rise to many trends during the twentieth century, from Latino supermodels to the music of Antonio Carlos Jobim, but the emergence of the flip-flop brand Havaianas as a global fashion phenomenon was perhaps the least expected. Since 1998 the simple rubber-soled thong sandals have been embellished with a small Brazilian flag (in celebration of the Brazilian football team's participation in that year's World Cup, which it did not in fact win), and this has come to represent one of the most ubiquitous and easily recognized brands in the world, with as many permutations and styles as there are fans.

The Havaianas company was founded in 1962 as part of South America's largest shoe manufacturer, the Alpargatas Group, and its shoes were originally inspired by the traditional Japanese *zori*, which has fabric straps and rice-straw soles. The textured, rice-shaped markings still found on the soles of every pair of Havaianas are a nod to the shoes' origins.

Within a year of their launch, Havaianas were selling at a rate of 1000 pairs a day; they were the cheapest footwear available in Brazil, often costing less than a dollar. Such was the demand, and so immediately assimilated into the South American way of life were they, that in the 1980s the Brazilian government began to count them as a shopping-basket staple, regulating their price along-side that of such items as bread and milk in order to control inflation.

Since their inception, Havaianas have come to express the very spirit and vitality of Brazil. Not only are they democratic, and worn by almost every-one of almost any class in the country, but also their flat rubber soles have become a blank canvas. Whether multi-coloured or plain, patterned or illustrated, Havaianas can be customized or initialled, reworked and reinvented by every wearer. The Brazilian actor Chico Anysio advertised the brand in the 1970s, by which time other companies were already intent on copying its runaway success, with the slogan 'Havaianas. The real ones'.

By the 1990s this slogan had become 'Havaianas. Everyone wears them', and the arrival of South American supermodels, such as Gisele Bündchen, on Western

The breadth of styles and designs is endless; from jewelled to embellished – even graffiti-ed – there is a model to suit all tastes. That, combined with accessible prices, has helped to make Havaianas an international megabrand.

catwalks ensured that the spotlight was on Brazil. In the wake of fashion's taste for 'heroin chic', the late 1990s saw an explosion of colour, bling and status-marking in brand identity, and Havaianas played a large part. Suddenly, even beyond Brazil, if one was wearing flip-flops, they had to be from the right label. While Havaianas may have been inexpensive in their native country, Europeans were prepared to pay ten times more to be seen in the right pair.

The company went from strength to strength: figures released in 2011 show that more than 50,000 Havaianas are sold every day, and six pairs are made every second. (By the time you finish reading this page, six more pairs will have been sold.) By 2010 the company was branching out into other types of footwear, creating trainers, hi-tops and espadrilles in the same colourful vein as its original flip-flops (opposite). It launched 'baby Havaianas' in 1997; since 2003 it has sponsored the Oscars ceremony and added its shoes to the attendees' gift bags; and in 2004 the Brazilian jeweller H. Stern collaborated on a special-edition pair, encrusted with diamonds and finished with 18-carat gold, costing more than £12,000.

The year 2006 saw the introduction of a gender-specific 'slim' range for women, in which the footpad was more contoured and the thong straps were narrower. Modifications of a design classic are not normally well received, but the collection has since become one of Havaianas' best-selling ranges.

In 2009 São Paulo was chosen as the location of Espaço Havaianas, a conceptual flagship store that also functions as a place of pilgrimage for aficionados of the brand.

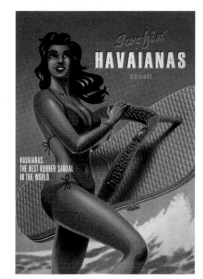

It carries many never-before-seen archival pieces, as well as housing a mini brand museum, and stocks several international limited-edition models that never made it on to the shelves in Brazil. It also sells newly developed models and offers a customization service, where one chooses colours and patterns for soles and uppers. In this haven for footwear enthusiasts, each wall is covered in flip-flops of every size in gradated colours, ranging from white to black, with every shade in between.

In some ways, Havaianas are the ultimate cult shoe: they are not a status symbol from any economic perspective, but simply a cultural one. Their rise and rise is not because of celebrity endorsement, but rather because of what they imply about a beach-centric, relaxed lifestyle. Many people are obsessed with them, and it's easy to see why: there is a lot going on behind that incredibly simple triumph of design.

Jimmy Choo

When Jimmy Choo founded his eponymous label with the then accessories editor of British *Vogue*, Tamara Mellon, in 1996, he had already been plying his trade for ten years. Although his creations had enjoyed the patronage of Diana, Princess of Wales, as well as exposure in the style press (in 1988 he had featured in a record eight pages of *Vogue*), his was still a niche name, and he was still working out of a studio in an old hospital building in Hackney, east London.

Having made his first pair of shoes at the age of eleven, Malaysian Choo (born 1961) supported himself throughout his time at Cordwainers, London, by working in restaurants and as a cleaner in a shoe factory, before graduating in 1983. He met Mellon on the PR and fashion circuit during the late 1980s, and she later persuaded him of the viability of high-end designer accessories. Together (and with money loaned by Mellon's father, a businessman) they built one of the first globally successful luxury shoe brands, known for selling some of the world's most expensive shoes.

The Jimmy Choo brand identity is one of hyper-femininity and unabashed

Jimmy Choo worked as a shoe designer for ten years before setting up his eponymous label. Pictured here are Marlene (opposite), Ava (above, left) and Anita.

Jimmy Choos have become the go-to footwear for red-carpet dressing, thanks to the label's reputation for classic but striking, unashamedly feminine styles, as well as boundless luxury. Shown here are Shirley (right) and Raquel.

opulence. Shoes drip with tassels, feathers and beads, and are made from every fabric imaginable. Choo himself left the company in 2001, selling his 50 per cent stake for £10 million, but he continues to work under licence from the company on the exclusive and bespoke Jimmy Choo Couture range. In Malaysia, the Sultan of Pahang conferred the honorary title 'Dato' on him in 2000, and he received an OBE for services to the shoe and fashion industry in 2002.

Under the direction of Tamara Mellon, the company continued to expand and began producing handbags, belts and eyewear, launching its first fragrance in 2011 and following that with a collection of men's footwear in the autumn of that year. Mellon herself was made an OBE in 2010 and, after the sale of the company to luxury-goods firm Labelux in May 2011 (Mellon made £85 million from the £525.5 million sale), stood down as director along with the chief executive, Joshua Schulman. She remains a creative consultant for the label.

Jimmy Choo first entered the mass consciousness through the television series *Sex and the City* (see p. 103), in which the principal character, Carrie Bradshaw (played by Sarah Jessica Parker), announced that it was one of her favourite boutiques. In a later episode, Bradshaw's cry of 'I lost my Choo!' caused both the label and its wares to become part of the fashion vernacular. The model worn by the character was the Feather shoe, a strappy platform sandal decorated with tiered peacock-feather edging. The label was also referred to in the film *The Devil Wears Prada* (2006), a supposed glimpse behind the scenes at the world's most infamous style

Far left and centre Scarlett Johansson at the premiere of *The Island*, London, August 2005; Emma Watson at the premiere of *My Week with Marilyn*, London, November 2011.

Left, top and bottom Fringing, feathers and fantastical flourishes are a Jimmy Choo signature; these shoes are Marlene (top) and Brigitte.

Below, left and centre The Duchess of Cambridge at the National Portrait Gallery, London, February 2012; Diana, Princess of Wales at the Royal Albert Hall, London, June 1997.

magazine. 'You sold your soul when you put on your first pair of Jimmy Choos', one character tells the heroine, the label itself by now famous enough to carry connotations of an insider level of fashion awareness.

The brand's reputation was cemented with a conspicuously popular collaboration with the Swedish high-street chain H&M in 2009, when footwear bearing the Jimmy Choo hallmarks sold in the United Kingdom for £150 (compared to mainline prices of more than £800). Further partnerships, with Wellington boot brand Hunter and sheepskin bootie maker UGG (pp. 181–85), ensured the aspirational nature of the label, while giving it an accessibility and attainability that many luxury brands lack.

This potent compound of prestige and popularity, combined with a USP of un-ashamed glamour, is the secret to the success of Jimmy Choo. Its shoes are fundamentally objects of desire, playing on perceptions of opulence and grandeur while always considering current trends and tastes. In celebration of the label's fifteenth anniversary, a capsule collection entitled 'Icons' was released in June 2011. 'I wanted to create a modern capsule collection inspired by memorable styles from our history that represented milestone moments for the brand and embody the DNA of our house style', said Mellon at the time. 'These modern interpretations of classic designs represent the iconic glamour of Jimmy Choo today.'[1]

Part of the collection was the Feather shoe; the Carly zebra-print boot, originally created to commemorate the brand's entry into American markets in 1998; the Macy, an ankle-strapped sandal and red-carpet

favourite worn by such actresses as Natalie Portman and Reese Witherspoon; and Fleur, a classic pointy-toed court shoe worn by Tamara Mellon as she collected her OBE.

Ten per cent of the profits from the Icons collection were donated to the Jimmy Choo Foundation, a charity set up by Mellon to champion the interests of women in developing countries. It has helped victims of rape in South Africa and donated more than $3.5 million to women in Africa affected by HIV. Choo himself is involved in setting up a shoemaking institute in Malaysia, to inspire budding designers to follow in his illustrious, and opulent, footsteps.

1. Quoted in 'Jimmy Choo Launches Icons Capsule Collection', Jimmy Choo website, undated; chooconnection.jimmychoo.com/content/jimmy-choo-launches-icons-capsule-collection (accessed June 2012).

Kurt Geiger

Kurt Geiger is a high-street success story that combines the heritage of an artisanal producer with the accessibility, reach and mass production of a megabrand. It is now Europe's largest luxury shoe retailer, but the first outpost was established on Bond Street when Geiger himself (born 1931) arrived in London from Austria in 1963. Twelve years later, in 1975, the brand's comfortable but stylish, fashion-forward footwear was introduced at House of Fraser, during a period of middle-class expansion when customers' horizons were broadening. By 1977 Geiger's designs were stocked in Harrods, too – where they remain today – as well as in Selfridges, John Lewis and Liberty.

After merging in 1978 with the shoe brand Carvela, which provided an even wider customer base, Kurt Geiger was acquired by House of Fraser, which in turn merged with Harrods in 1994. These shifts made no difference to the popularity and integrity of the brand, and high-street shoppers were still eager to buy its affordable versions of high-end styles, as well as its own inimitable takes on the trends of the day. By securing so many outposts across the country,

Opposite Gwen.

Above Ladybell.

Left The original Kurt Geiger shop opened on Bond Street, London, but the brand now has stores across the United Kingdom and the world, with recent branches opening in Russia and Qatar.

Kurt Geiger soon became a leading name in women's footwear and paved the way for a broader high-street revolution, as the democratizing of fashion became something of an economic and political trope.

In 1995 the company launched its men's collection, which has since taken a place of similar prominence in its own sphere, providing smart and well-made work shoes, as well as – in recent years – more sports-inspired, casual pieces. In 1997 the diffusion line KG*Kurt Geiger was launched, to attract a younger market in order that they might grow into the mainline as they matured. KG models are characterized by an attention to seasonal trends and plenty of colour, with platforms and embellishment taking centre stage at the time of writing.

After opening a concept boutique on London's South Molton Street in 2001, the company took charge of its own supply chain in 2004, and Barclays Private Equity supported a management buy-out of the company in 2005. An in-house design team was added to the staff, in order that the brand might focus on honing its aesthetic and its reputation for quality. It also expanded overseas during this period, with a franchise opening in the Middle East and in department stores in Paris and Milan, where the competition of native footwear brands had previously seemed too stiff to negotiate.

A second management buy-out saw Graphite Capital take charge in 2009 in a deal worth £95 million, and the first task of

Inspired by the latest catwalk trends, Kurt Geiger offers directional footwear at the upper end of the high-street price bracket. Pictured here are Class (right), Enigma (below) and Lancelotte (opposite).

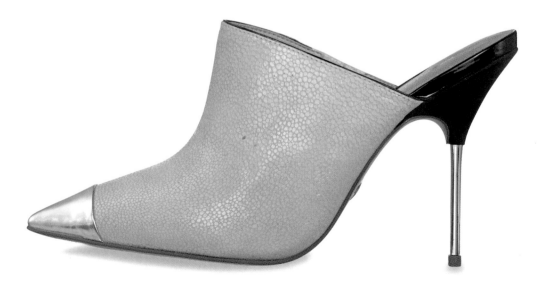

the new owners was to focus on grass-roots customers of the sort that had always been loyal to Kurt Geiger. Stores in Liverpool and London's Covent Garden were redeveloped. After two years Graphite sold Kurt Geiger to the footwear-based Jones Group, an American company that owns the shoe brand Nine West, making a profit of £120 million in June 2011.

'I'd be very disappointed if we didn't see Kurt Geiger opening in America next year', the chief executive, Neil Clifford, said at the time. 'Jones Group is huge in America – they've got 700 stores [there], while we've got none, and we've never had the bottle to try it before. We've had a brilliant ride with private equity but now we'd like to park the company for the long term and not look over our shoulders every three or four years. It's been a great journey but we now want to think about the next ten years.'[1]

Months after this news was announced, Kurt Geiger launched a collection called 'Everything But the Dress', which extended its line of accessories into bags and purses, and reached out to its roots once more with the opening of a new store on Grafton Street, Mayfair, a stone's throw from the site of Geiger's original Bond Street premises.

There has been expansion, too, with more than twenty-four standalone Kurt Geiger stores now open across Britain – including lucrative spots in several airports – and new outlets in Russia, Turkey, Dubai, Kuwait, Qatar and Bahrain. The launch of a newly revamped internet presence and a new offer of international shipping for online orders announce the next chapter in a brand that has been a constant in the recent history of the footwear trade.

1. Quoted in Tom Bawden and Zoe Wood, 'Kurt Geiger Sale to Jones Group Means £20m Windfall for Shoe-chain Managers', *The Guardian*, 2 June 2011; guardian.co.uk/business/2011/jun/02/kurt-geiger-sold-jones-group (accessed March 2012).

Manolo Blahnik

Roger Vivier (pp. 145–47) may have been known as the Stiletto King, but it was Manolo Blahnik who brought that razor-sharp style back from the sartorial wilderness in the 1970s. At a time when wedges and platforms were de rigueur, the young designer focused on the spindly aesthetic that had been more prevalent in footwear during the 1950s, when Vivier's couture styles reigned supreme. Blahnik focused on footwear because he had been told to: in 1970, as a fledgling shop assistant and writer for *Vogue Italia*, he showed a portfolio of his fashion designs to the then editor-in-chief of US *Vogue*, the indomitable Diana Vreeland, who told him that shoes must be his concern. The following year, the designer Ossie Clark asked Blahnik to create the shoes for his catwalk show and, amid exotic styles with clutches of cherries at the ankle (right), a brand was born.

Blahnik (born Manuel Blahnik Rodríguez to a Czech father and Spanish mother in 1942) was raised in the Canary Islands. He moved to London in 1968 and eventually bought the boutique for which he worked, Zapata on Old Church Street in Chelsea, opening it under his own name.

Opposite Amiela.

Far left Sketch of shoe for Christian Dior catwalk show, 1997.

Left Manolo Blahnik, 2011.

Below Sketch of Ivy for Ossie Clark catwalk show, 1971.

It attracted the likes of Jane Birkin and Lauren Bacall, and in 1987 Blahnik cracked the American market with a collection for Bloomingdale's.

Blahnik has worked on such films as *The Hunger* (1983), starring Catherine Deneuve, and Sofia Coppola's MTV-generation take on the life of Marie Antoinette (2006), in which his baroque, bejewelled and buckled creations settled against the backdrop of Versailles as if they were destined for such elegant surroundings. This has made Blahnik something of a celebrity among shoe designers, with fans queueing for hours to meet him, and various accolades – such as a plaque on the Walk of Style on Rodeo Drive, Los Angeles – being handed to him. In a rather more sober ceremony, Blahnik was made a CBE in 2007 for services to the British fashion industry. He has also been named Accessory Designer of the Year twice by the British Fashion Council, in 1990 and 1999.

It was the editor of *Vogue*, Anna Wintour, who coined the abbreviation 'Manolos' during the mid-1980s, and Blahnik's cult of personality was born when the super-models Christy Turlington and Linda Evangelista admitted that they had each purchased a pair of his heels and his flats, 'for running between shows'. In 1994 Diana, Princess of Wales wore a pair to an event the night Prince Charles admitted his affair with Camilla Parker-Bowles on national television.

Since then the name Manolo has become associated with a certain style of ultra-luxurious and high-end footwear, with an upmarket identity formed in the homes of the wealthy in New York's Chelsea and

Opposite Hangisi.

Left, from top Campari; Culona.

celebrity. I am not a movie star or a football player, I just do my thing. If I sell, good, if I don't, well, I try to do something about it.'[1] But the truth is that he has a coterie of followers who will always buy his shoes. For all the colourful and jazzy design tics, there are just as many neutral and timeless classics in a shape that Blahnik himself has ensured will never be out of style again.

Blahnik has also rehabilitated the notion of the shoe designer as craftsman, an artisan working according to his own code in his own workshop, rather than producing shoes for the megabrands and corporations of the world simply as a sideline. In this respect, he paved the way for the likes of Christian Louboutin, Nicholas Kirkwood and Pierre Hardy (pp. 43–48, 117–21 and 123–27), returning the role of shoe designer to something closer to what it was during Roger Vivier's day.

Upper East Side. Blahnik has found his way into popular culture easily, becoming shorthand for the sort of cult footwear made accessible by such shows as *Sex and the City* (see opposite). The protagonist is a specific name-dropper in that respect; when confronted by a mugger, she readily hands over her bag and jewellery before he spots her most lucrative possession. 'Your Manolo Blahniks', he demands, gesturing at her feet with a gun.

'I feel ambiguous about it', Blahnik told *The Independent* in 2008 of *Sex and the City*. 'It has [made] me this kind of icon, Madonna kind of thing, which I am really not. I never wanted to be the most famous, the most beautiful, most extravagant. This kind of thing has almost forced me to be more detached from the machine of

In common with Vivier, Blahnik created the footwear for Christian Dior couture shows, in his case under the direction of the designer John Galliano: 'When I worked … on shoes for the … couture shows, it was extraordinary because [John's] mind was like wildfire, but it's difficult to work with the machine. I think I am one of the smallest surviving brands.' Blahnik works alone, sketching his designs for a small team of people who produce them in family-run factories; he has no formal training. But he has conquered the world of footwear, and his name is one that demands top billing whenever it is discussed.

1. Quoted in Carola Long, 'Well-heeled: A Rare Audience with Manolo Blahnik', *The Independent*, 27 September 2008; independent.co.uk/943446.html (accessed March 2012). All subsequent quotations are from this source.

Sex and the City

If there is one person who can be credited with changing the way shoes are perceived beyond specialist circles, it is Carrie Bradshaw of *Sex and the City* (1998–2004). The wise-talking, wise-typing fictitious heroine of the HBO television series based on an anthology of columns by the writer Candace Bushnell (1997) inspired much latterday footwear fetishism with her highly prized and extensive collection of luxury shoes from labels that have since become part of the vernacular.

Manolo Blahnik and Jimmy Choo (pp. 99–102 and 87–91), in particular, were popularized in this way, and were made household names by episodes in which Bradshaw (played by Sarah Jessica Parker, above, second from left) is respectively held at gunpoint for her stilettos and misses the last ferry home because of a heel stuck in an iron grating. 'I lost my Choo!' she cries at the departing boat, succinctly placing the Malaysian designer in the celluloid hall of fame.

These were far from Bradshaw's only go-to labels, of course: she also wore heels by Brian Atwood, Pierre Hardy (pp. 123–27) and Christian Dior, among others. But it was her idolizing of shoe designers that gave credence to a new way of viewing fashionable footwear,

not to mention a new attitude to spending money on designer brands.

As Bradshaw kept her heels boxfresh and wrapped in tissue paper, so did her fans. Shoes became a symbol not of wealth (although prices were high) but of fashionability itself, of being label-conscious and engaged to a level that had previously been expected only of those who worked in the industry. Designer names entered common parlance, becoming a currency among those who paid to show they knew what they were talking about.

It was during the airing of the series that shoes became a specifically gynocentric device. With Bradshaw as its figurehead, footwear became a barometer of glamour as clothing had previously been. Shoes became a totem for the modern woman, an empowering aspect of fashion that did not relate to body size or body-consciousness. After all, so the maxim went, you're never too fat for your shoes. Bradshaw was the first shoe obsessive of popular culture, and every other woman seemed to follow: her mania for shoe shopping became an international habit.

It is very likely that *Sex and the City* had an effect on the price of fashionable footwear, too, considering the characters' constant salving of

each other's conscience after spending hundreds of dollars on designer shoes. One episode relates the shoe obsessive's ethic with particular emphasis. 'A Woman's Right to Shoes', first broadcast in 2003, tells the story of a pair of silver Manolo Blahniks stolen from a child's birthday party when the hostess asks Bradshaw to remove them. On offering to pay her back, the hostess discovers that they cost $400, and declares this to be ridiculous. Bradshaw is adamant that, as an unmarried woman with no children, shoes are her due in lieu of engagement, wedding or children's presents, and eventually the hostess buys another pair as a gift to celebrate Bradshaw's engagement – to herself. The episode goes so far as to depict high-end shoe boutiques as places where children are not welcome, underscoring the importance of footwear to a certain demographic of independent, sartorially aware women.

If it is the designer who imbues shoes with an identity and aesthetic, it is Bradshaw who personifies the ethics of buying and wearing them, and who invented the notion of treating them as a commodity.

Melissa

One of the key selling points of the footwear brand Melissa is that its signature jelly shoes come with an unmistakable candy-like scent – designed, the company insists, to remind us of our childhood. If that sounds a little offbeat and quirky, then it encapsulates Melissa's market identity perfectly. Although the Brazilian label has existed since 1971, it is only since 2000 that it has really shot to prominence after collaborations with some of fashion's most conspicuous and high-end names. It has become one of the largest and most successful footwear brands in the world, with an annual income of more than $1 billion, and more than 600 products released every year. It sells more than 170 million pairs of shoes annually in more than 50 countries, and it employs almost 30,000 people worldwide. Who said plastic shoes can't be chic?

But, despite this success, Melissa is not about big business in the traditional sense of the phrase. It has built its identity and global presence through the development and use of ethical techniques and strategies that are designed to chime with the international need to cut emissions and

Opposite Collaboration with Gareth Pugh.

Left In the Galeria Melissa, São Paulo, Brazil. *Afromania* by Pier Balestrieri (top) and *Urban Art* by Choque Cultural (Culture Shock) gallery, São Paulo.

save resources. Melissa's credentials are apparent in its use of Melflex, a singularly malleable form of PVC developed in-house, from which all its shoes are made. (The unusual sweetshop fragrance is perhaps intended to counter the rather pungent smell of industrially produced acetates.)

The brand thrives on collaboration or, as the company dubs it, 'partnership', first undertaken during the 1980s. The company holds various licences to produce footwear emblazoned with images of Disney characters and Smurfs, for example, but it also works with Brazilian celebrities, such as the singer Lovefoxxx (who topped off her jelly sandals with a large plastic rat). Other collaborations have been with the Brazilian design duo Fernando and Humberto Campana, and the Italian architect Gaetano Pesce.

Working with architects has been key to Melissa's evolution. The brand's creative director and head of research and development, Edson Matsuo, studied the discipline, a fact that is obvious in the company's

striving to reinvent and push the boundaries of the jelly shoe. A partnership with Zaha Hadid in 2008 saw the prize-winning architect emulate the fluid, sinuous style of her buildings in a pair of Möbius strip-style latticed jelly booties. 'The fluidity of our design was a perfect fit for Melissa's plastic technology, injecting seamless pieces', Hadid said.[1]

One of the first collaborations to bring Melissa to the attention of European buyers was with Vivienne Westwood in 2009, re-creating forty-five of her most iconic footwear styles according to the Brazilian firm's plastic specifications. The Lady Dragon sandals, complete with kitten heel and flippy heart, were a widespread success, and Westwood was a vocal exponent of Melissa's eco credentials. 'It's quite unusual what Melissa can do with plastic', she said at the time. 'Each shoe has a character and tells a story.'[2] Among other classic Westwood shoes to be given the Melissa treatment were her infamous geisha-esque Rocking Horse

Opposite, from top
J.W. Ultragirl; Wanting Lace.

Above Cristal.

Below Peace.

Opposite, **from top** Aileron;
J.W. Lady Dragon.

winged platform sandals and a pair of rubber galoshes decorated with three plastic buttons.

Melissa has also worked with such designers as the couturier Jean Paul Gaultier, who produced a strappy, nail-heeled stiletto that defied expectations of the form; the designer Gareth Pugh, whose black-and-white booties are reminiscent of his neo-gothic catwalk looks; and the maximalist virtuoso Thierry Mugler, who created a pair of metallic bronze pumps for the company in 1983.

Melissa has sponsored many young designers, who also receive support and mentoring. The Melissa Academy holds workshops for students of design globally, with the aim of engineering new developments in the field and of creating new styles for the brand. Several have since gone into production, including a metallic gold heel, supported at its base by a plastic rendering of a rubber duck.

As a member of the Council of Fashion Designers of America (CFDA) since 2012, Melissa holds an important position in retail in the United States, with more than 1000 outlets in the country. A recent partnership with the designer Jason Wu, who was made famous by the patronage of First Lady Michelle Obama, and who won the CFDA womenswear award in 2010, yielded delicate jelly ballet slippers decorated with digitally printed lace and arabesque designs (p. 106).

The first Melissa shoe to be produced in the 1970s was the Spider, a black plastic woven style with a flat sole. Nowadays, the classic Aranha is generally considered to be the company's most popular design; a weft-topped jelly sandal in a rainbow of different colours, it takes just one minute to be produced on the conveyor belt.

1. Quoted by Melissa press office.
2. *Ibid.*

Marro's idiosyncratic sense of design has ensured that her creations have been noticed by dedicated and directional taste-makers, such as Lady Gaga. Pictured below are court shoes with ankle spats (left) and heel-less ankle boots with Swarovski crystals, both in mint-green semi-patent leather, and both created for the singer.

Marro's design aesthetic. Each pair of Natacha Marro shoes is unusual, not just for the fact that it is a collector's item fitted to a single foot, but also because all her shoes are multidimensional and hyperbolic in their aspect – heel-less, often, or exaggerated in their vertiginous height; sometimes impossible to walk in, or macabre; but always perfectly calibrated to the wearer and the effect they had in mind. 'I love creating the perfect shoes for the right person', she says. 'Something that works only for that individual and no one else – it can be very simple or very complicated.'

Many of Marro's shoes are wedges, with platforms and soles concealed behind wrapped leather or skin to create an almost hoof-like shape. In fact, she once designed a pair of platform cloven hooves for a customer. Since creating shoes for an exhibition in 1995, she has risen to a certain level of conspicuousness in the fashion industry, and has made footwear for such films as *Star Wars: Episode I: The Phantom Menace* (1999), in which her pieces were worn by Ewan McGregor and Liam Neeson, and for album covers, such as Erasure's *Cowboy* (1997).

Throughout the 1990s Marro's designs were also appearing in underground style magazines, such as *The Face* and *Pure Magazine*, as well as being featured as fetish gear in *Time Out*. Superstars including David Bowie and Gwen Stefani, as well as such subcultural icons as Grace Jones and Grayson Perry, have commissioned shoes from Marro; she has also dressed the feet of Judy Garland, Marilyn Monroe and Marlene Dietrich, albeit by proxy, by creating footwear for their lookalikes in the waxworks museum Madame Tussaud's.

Marro works with unexpected and esoteric materials, such as calf- and ponyskin and alligator, to create shoes that defy not only expectations, but also gravity.

Marro's idiosyncratic heel-less design was inspired by subcultural bondage designs, and has been copied by the mainstream.

Marro opened her first store in 2000, surprised by the demand for bespoke shoes. But there is a market for one-off footwear, a trend that has blossomed further with the appearance of Lady Gaga. 'It has been like an explosion', Marro says of her work with Stefani Germanotta (Lady Gaga's real name). '[She is] the opposite of every customer! Usually people want something flattering, something to match their dress or so on, but no – with her it is about doing something completely different, against any rules. You can go as far as you can. I love it.' Pieces she has designed for the megastar include a pair of pistachio-green leather platforms in her trademark front-weighted and cantilevered style, with pointed, rhinestone-embellished toes that extend beyond the frontal platforms, as well as suede panelling and Achilles lacing at the heel (p. 112). Another pair features the cartoonish platforms and pencil-thin heels of a Jessica Rabbit-type ideal, again rendered in pistachio leather, with a miniature gaiter that laces behind the leg for a bodice effect.

Marro also retains a permanent collection of off-the-peg shoes, including now-iconic styles of Mary-Janes – again subverted with a cartoonish fuller frontal platform and spindly heels, fastened by ribbons at the front – and a knee-high corset boot (opposite, left), with a 5- or 6-inch (12.5- or 15-cm) heel. Bestsellers among these varieties include her thigh-high models, made from leather or rubber, and her 'can-can' boots, a laced style inspired by the stomping stagegirls of the Wild West.

Natacha Marro deals in fantasy, to the extent that many of her styles are synonymous with the fetish scene or other extremes

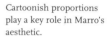
Cartoonish proportions play a key role in Marro's aesthetic.

of subculture: she makes shoes for dominatrices and those who reinvent themselves. It is a mark, perhaps, of how much a part of the mainstream the design quirks of such subcultures have become that Marro's shoes now reach such a wide audience.

'I didn't really have much of a reference for women's shoes,' Marro explains, 'because I mainly wore men's shoes until I was about twenty years old. So, when I started wearing heels, I tried to create something I really wanted to wear, and it felt as though I could do something more original because I felt free from all these references in my mind.'

1. All quotations from Natacha Marro are taken from email correspondence with the author, December 2011–February 2012.

Nicholas Kirkwood

Nicholas Kirkwood (born 1980) is one of the world's most important young shoe designers. His signature stilettos, complete with trademark recessive platform on the instep, have become items of cult desire and copying, creating for the footwear world a new silhouette that has essentially gone viral. 'Inspiration can come from anywhere,' he says, 'but the general thing is that I start with organic [forms] mixed with architectural [ones], then layer on seasonal inspirations. This winter [2012–13] is probably the first time I've tried to put a real theme across the entire collection. It's from the movie *Midnight in Paris* [2011], bringing the people and the elements of that time [the 1920s] into the shoes. But it actually started off with the Pre-Raphaelites.'[1]

There is a sinuous and fluid beauty to Kirkwood's designs, the frilled uppers of which often feature laser-cut Art Deco shapes, fins and quilled straps, and are rarely trimmed with extraneous elements. While not specifically minimalist in his approach, Kirkwood aims to make a statement with the curvilinear forms of his work, rather than with excessive adornment. His

Nicholas Kirkwood's designs marry high femininity and classic design with innovation and sculptural ambition.

Kirkwood is inspired by the angularity and straight lines of modern architecture and sculpture.

shoes have become the footwear of choice for the directional crowd, the cognoscenti, to wear to high-profile events – and the shoes are conspicuous for their character-istic profiles and delicately structural qualities, which aim to marry masculine and feminine attributes.

'It's about trying to explore new shapes and interesting materials', Kirkwood continues. '[My work] has to have that sense of the unexpected – I definitely play a lot with proportions. I love the mix of light and heavy together. They can be day shoes but are probably more likely to be an evening shoe – not necessarily red carpet, but probably not for the office.' His modernist take on formal footwear is, however, sweetly nostalgic in its sense of decoration and femininity; reference is made not to the hard geometry of Bauhaus purism but instead to the sweeping curlicues of the *fin de siècle*. And his style retains a sense of the femininity of that era: opulent and delicate but also complex and strong.

Kirkwood launched his own collection in spring 2005 after graduating from Cordwainers, London, and quickly won the attention of such muses and style icons as Grace Jones, Daphne Guinness and Isabella Blow for his originality of thought. In 2006 he was awarded the Condé Nast/*Footwear News* Vivian Infantino award for emerging talent. By 2007 he had also won the prestigious AltaRoma/*Vogue Italia* award (for his Spring/Summer 2008 collection), and came highly recommended by fashion soothsayers Franca

Sozzani, editor of *Vogue Italia*, and André Leon Talley, American *Vogue*'s editor-at-large. The Spring/Summer collection of 2008 was characterized by the inclusion of a sub-genre of successful evening shoes and the beginning of a partnership between Kirkwood and the crystal company Swarovski. In 2008 Kirkwood won not only the British Fashion Award for Emerging Talent (accessories) but also the Condé Nast/*Footwear News* Designer of the Year gong, and the following year he opened his first standalone concession in London's ultra-high-end and avant-garde concept store Dover Street Market (owned by Comme des Garçons designer Rei Kawakubo).

As well as producing his own range, Kirkwood is now creative director for the Italian shoe brand Pollini, a name that had its heyday in the 1970s and '80s with its glamorous technicolour designs, but which has lately fallen off the fashion radar. Kirkwood's appointment has led to several collaborations with the avant-garde, including knee-high PVC polka-dot boots for the catwalk show of the designer Louise Gray, and the introduction of a distinctive wavy platform sole. Kirkwood has restored some of the label's previous fame with sturdy wedges and preppy loafers that have found a home in some of the most forward-thinking publications of the style press. 'I didn't want Pollini to be just another sexy Italian shoe brand – there's a million and one of those', he explains. 'I wanted to give a slightly less obvious feel, but one that's immediately identifiable. Or will be, with time.'

Kirkwood has also created catwalk footwear for such labels as Rodarte and Erdem. This sort of 'show shoe' rarely

Kirkwood's shoes are both conservative and creative, and retain a sense of practicality and wearability. Exotic skins and luxe materials are important to their sense of high-end cool.

While Kirkwood's designs may share a classic elegance, the designer is not scared to use colour boldly or to riff on inspiration from modern visual culture.

makes it into production, but is intended to represent the collection itself, a dramatic piece of design to help the label assimilate seasonal character – a dramatic device, even. But such was the demand for Kirkwood's stone-inspired stilettos for Rodarte, twisted with studs and decorated with a cloud-like fog from the label's apocalypse-inspired Spring/Summer 2010 collection, that limited numbers went on sale in such stores as Barneys New York and Harvey Nichols. In the same way, the digitally printed silk hiking boots with a 6-inch (15-cm) heel designed for Erdem's Autumn/Winter 2010–11 collection sold out at such boutiques as London's Matches.

Much of Kirkwood's success comes from his innovative use of unusual materials, such as devoré satin, hand-printed suede and leather, and shaved stingray. Python crops up, too, as do rubberized leather, cobra and alligator, if further proof were needed that Kirkwood's designs work to a similarly rarified version of luxury as does couture footwear.

1. All quotations from Nicholas Kirkwood are taken from email correspondence with the author, December 2011–February 2012.

Personal sketches from Kirkwood's design studio.

Pierre Hardy

The Paris-based designer Pierre Hardy is almost singular in his rejection of fashion history. When it comes to finding inspiration for his architectural, graphic, industrial-looking footwear, he turns to conceptual art and logic, writing codes and creating formulae for each style, carefully calibrating pressure and mass, using the physical laws of gravity and equilibrium to create objects of desire.

'I always try to bring something new [to my designs] in the most radical way I can', Hardy explains. 'My inspiration comes from very different things that look beautiful to me. But the inspiration, almost always, comes from an area that is far from fashion. It can be objects, places, art, but it's seldom a character or a fantasy story.'[1]

Witness the Lego shoe, which Hardy developed with Balenciaga's creative director, Nicolas Ghesquière, for the label's Autumn/Winter 2007–08 collection (he has collaborated with Balenciaga since 2001), grown from snowboard bindings that he spotted in a New York ski store; or his Skyline sandal, with its head-scratching clusters of metallic rectangles. Hardy's mastery of skyscraper heels and his talent

Hardy's work for his own label and the house of Balenciaga is informed by an interest in structural and severe modernism, softened by his choice of palette and finish. Pictured here are shoes from Spring/Summer 2009 (opposite) and Autumn/Winter 2011–12.

Hardy's influences come from architecture and modern art schools, such as Bauhaus and De Stijl, as seen in these shoes (clockwise from right) from Spring/Summer 2006, Autumn/Winter 2009–10, Autumn/Winter 2011–12, Spring/Summer 2008, Autumn/Winter 2007–08 and Spring/Summer 2005.

for innovation are at the heart of the increasingly complex tastes and trends in modern-day shoe design.

'With Pierre, there is always a potent mix of historical knowledge and the ultra-contemporary', Ghesquière told *Elle* in 2011. 'And a great spectrum of inspirations – it could be modernism, design, art, but most importantly, everything is totally twenty-first century.'[2]

'I try to find the balance between creativity and reality', says Hardy. 'First it has to surprise you, even shock you, and then it has to seduce you. Pure lines, sculptural shapes and architectural volumes. I try to make it as clean as possible, and not to mix things together too much, avoiding useless detail.'

Hardy was born and bred in Paris, a student of contemporary dance before studying fine art at the city's prestigious École Normale Supérieure. He then became a fashion illustrator for such titles as *Vogue Homme* and *Vanity Fair*, but was poached in 1987 to create women's shoes for Christian Dior. In 1990 he moved to the world's most luxurious leather-goods house, Hermès, working as creative director first for women's and then for men's shoes, before becoming creative director of fine jewellery in 2001. Hardy launched his own women's footwear label in 1999, following with men's shoes in 2002 and bags in 2006. Since 2003 he has shown his designs as part of the biannual collections in Paris at the Galerie de Valois in the gardens of the Palais-Royal.

Indeed, Hardy is so firmly a part of the French luxury tradition that in 2009 he was admitted to the Comité Colbert, an

aggregate of just seventy-five members founded in 1954 by Jean-Jacques Guerlain to promote the interests of the French luxury-goods trade. As if to declare his high-end credentials, in 2010 Hardy developed the 'haute jewellery' collection for Hermès, for which he famously designed a platinum riding-whip necklace studded with 3669 tiny diamonds and costing more than £580,000.

'I love the idea of "accompanying" a woman', Hardy says. 'Sometimes helping her to be herself, but better, and sometimes pushing her to be different. I'd like the women who are wearing my shoes to be strong but sensual at the same time.' And his aesthetic combines the two: severe straight lines are countered by the physicality of his designs. Rigid skyscraper heels come with cage-like leather straps and curvatures; block-heeled boots have soft leather uppers and concealed platforms; even the infamous Lego model was rendered feminine in the minute delicacy of the albeit chunky blocks from which it was constructed. Hardy's work is a constant conflict between drama and comfort; his expert understanding of physics means that, despite appearances, practicality is never far from the remit.

Hardy's widespread popularity is testament to that. Since 2007 he has been a creative consultant for the American high-street chain Gap, for which he has created a number of bestselling – indeed, sell-out – styles: sheepskin-lined suede buckled ankle boots; wooden-soled sandals with a tripartite tan-leather strap; and, more recently, elegantly bourgeois ankle-strapped court shoes – the high-street resurrection of the beleaguered pointed toe. Each is a design classic that insistently stands beyond any extant design movement.

'Creations are always like a dream, and my dreams are often oriented to the future', Hardy explains. 'I like the idea of construction, of colour blocks. My work is a mix of different focuses: scales, distortion, mechanics and structure on one hand, and on the other hand femininity, modernity, fluidity, movement and sensuality.'

Having won several awards, including a coveted prize for the best shoe design at the *Wallpaper** Design Awards in 2006, Hardy needs no endorsement, but the line-up of stars who wear his shoes regularly includes Nicole Kidman, Madonna, Uma Thurman and Charlotte Gainsbourg. 'Shoes tend to outlast more ephemeral effects', says Hardy of his famous followers. 'Their personalization brings a lot more cachet to the brand.'

1. All quotations from Pierre Hardy are taken from email correspondence with the author, December 2011–February 2012, unless otherwise stated.
2. Quoted in Christopher Bagley, 'The Genius of Pierre Hardy', *Elle*, 23 December 2011; elle.com/Fashion/Fashion-Spotlight/The-Genius-of-Pierre-Hardy (accessed June 2012).

Opposite Shoes from Spring/Summer 2008 (top left and bottom right); Autumn/Winter 2009–10 (top right and bottom left).

Far left Blue and red slingback from Spring/Summer 2012.

Left After plenty of celebrity exposure, as well as sell-out collaborations with the high-street retailer Gap, Pierre Hardy and his innovative and singular designs have joined the footwear hall of fame. Nicole Kidman (top) attends the Santa Barbara International Film Festival, February 2011; Leighton Meester is seen in Madrid, May 2010.

Below Spring/Summer 2009 (top); Spring/Summer 2012.

Pretty Ballerinas

Tradition and craft have combined with trend and taste to create the fashion success story that is Pretty Ballerinas. All its wares are still made on the island of Menorca by the Mascaro family, which has handled the manufacture of its ballet shoes since 1918; the company was launched under its current name in 2005. Those first models are still available, in muted shades of silk from oyster to Tahitian pearl, with the soft leather sole unchanged; but the brand's broader remit these days is to satisfy the widespread demand for ballet-style shoes that are sturdy enough to cope with everyday use.

Pretty Ballerinas offers a vast range of colours, designs, effects and styles, from different shapes and fits (all named after Hollywood stars, so that customers might more easily remember which one they feel suits them best) to low-rise uppers (which show more of the toes) and traditionally higher cut styles, as well as various heel heights. Customers can also choose from a variety of finishes and trims: grosgrain ribbon, satin edging, twisted silk strings and velvet. Patterns vary from leopard print to zebra, paisley and Liberty prints, in matte

Opposite Hannah (girl's shoe) in ivory satin with nude trim.

Left, from top Shirley in animal print with patent toecap; Marilyn, blue with white spots and red trim; Pretty Ballerinas store, Covent Garden, London.

or patent leather, or simply block colours of a Pantone variety.

Since opening its first boutique in London's Mayfair in 2007, Pretty Ballerinas has proliferated across Europe and the world, with stores in North and South America, its native Spain, Turkey, Taiwan and, most recently, Tel Aviv. These shops are designed to look like chocolate boxes: characteristically small, they present the myriad shoes coffret-style, with each variety laid out on shelves, backed by traditional shoe tins and boxes to imitate the authentic ballet-shoe experience. Indeed, in the breadth of choice and wealth of variety, Pretty Ballerinas is the closest thing to a bespoke footwear service for dancers that the average non-specialist consumer can expect to find.

In another modern flourish, the brand has also diversified into embellishments on its shoes. After the ballet-shoe trend was popularized as part of a bohemian renaissance emanating from the Primrose Hill set of north London, it was adopted by such high-end catwalk designers as Alber Elbaz of Lanvin and even Miuccia Prada, both of whom put their own spin on flat footwear clearly influenced by the dance tradition. While Prada's curling elasticated poulanes came in bold colours adorned with clusters of beads and costume jewels, the Lanvin styles took the beauty of classical ballet to newly elegant heights, adding curls of ribbon, loops of grosgrain and sparkling embellishment.

Pretty Ballerinas has done this on a mass-market scale, giving its ballet shoes pretty and witty additions that range from frills and flowers, hand-tooled from petals

of leather, to a red patent-leather Dalí-esque pair of lips and a red-leather guitar, the last two appearing on the same, rather surrealist pair of shoes.

This diversification and evolution prove the importance of trends in footwear. That there are only so many styles of shoe available at a layman's level – flat, heeled, open, closed, boot, sandal and so on – plays a large part in the creativity of designers, who push constantly to make these styles more and more individual. When one considers the ballet shoe, one might at first see it as exhausted, given that it has been reworked in so many different colours already. But the designers at Pretty Ballerinas see the ballet shoe as a blank canvas, and that is a great part of their products' ingenuity and charm.

PrettyBallerinas
COLLECTION 2008

Opposite and above Pretty Ballerinas has widened the appeal of the humble dance shoe by presenting it in a plethora of colours, along with collectible presentation tins and carry-cases.

Left This advertisement for Pretty Ballerinas from 2008 plays on the 'dance school' connotations of the brand and its roots in the dance industry.

There is also a strong sense of the need to remain up-to-date even when dealing with a style that is inherently traditional. Trend-focused initiatives by the company include the release of limited-edition packaging every season, ranging from collectors' metal tins moulded to the exact shape of the shoes to transparent acetate carry-bags and canvas totes. The inclusion, too, of prominent fashion bloggers in the firm's advertising campaigns and brand imagery has helped it to remain at the forefront of footwear trends. And, in 2009, Pretty Ballerinas launched its Young Princess collection for children, a range that was given the best possible exposure when the supermodel Kate Moss chose it for all sixteen of her young bridesmaids when she married Jamie Hince in August 2011 (above). Other celebrity fans of the brand include the models Elle Macpherson and Claudia Schiffer, as well as the singer Lily Allen and the actress Angelina Jolie.

Opposite The standard shape of the Pretty Ballerina shoe belies the extraordinary variety of materials, colours and trimmings in which it is available. All the shoes pictured here are Rosario, except second from top left (Miley) and bottom right (Shirley).

Above, left Kate Moss with her daughter, Lila Grace, and her other bridesmaids, all wearing shoes from the Young Princess collection, August 2011.

Above, centre and right Claudia Schiffer at the premiere of *Stardust*, October 2007; Princess Letizia of Spain at Club Nautico, Palma da Mallorca, August 2010.

Left Hannah (girl's shoe) in green patent leather with bumblebee and flower.

Repetto

I t is difficult to imagine a time when ballet pumps were not a fixture of everyday life. The flat-soled dance shoe has so long been a staple of fashionable footwear that it is odd to think that it was once precisely that – a dance shoe.

The French company Repetto is credited with facilitating the crossover. Its leather creations have adorned the feet of everyone from Kate Moss to Serge Gainsbourg and, most notably, Brigitte Bardot, first and foremost a trained dancer before she became an international sex symbol, and whose taste for Repetto pumps became a style statement in itself. In 1956 she asked Rose Repetto to create a shoe for her that was as delicate and comfortable as a dance flat but sturdy enough for everyday use, and in the film ... *And God Created Woman* of that year she teamed a pair of scarlet leather ballet pumps with cropped trousers and a Breton top to create the inimitable Gallic look.

Since then, ballet pumps have become de rigueur, but Repetto maintains that it is the idiosyncratic 'stitch and return' technique that makes its version the most durable. The pumps are created by stitching underneath the sole, before being turned

It was on the instructions of the dancer-turned-actress Brigitte Bardot that Repetto created a sturdy-soled version of its ballet slipper suited to everyday use.

Above Repetto has diversified its offering, moving into lace-ups and sandals, all recognizable for their simple elegance, fuss-free finish and the thin, flat soles normally found on dance shoes.

Below Advertising campaign for Spring/Summer 2012.

inside out. The leather uppers are stretched over a last and sewn to the thicker leather sole; when the pumps are inversed, the technique produces a near-invisible join between sole and upper.

Repetto was founded in 1947 by matriarch Rose Repetto (1880–1980), whose choreographer son, Roland Petit, persuaded her to start a dance-shoe workshop. Soon such great names as Rudolf Nureyev and Eric Vu-An were visiting her boutique on the rue de la Paix in Paris. The brand still makes professional dance shoes, and is one of very few companies left that supply custom-fit models to ballet dancers. There are more than 150 dancers on its books, each of whom needs up to three pairs of shoes for every evening's performance, as the silk of an authentic ballet shoe often tears under the rigours of the discipline. The Repetto Foundation also supplies dance shoes to numerous dance schools and academies around the world. 'Our roots are in the dance world. This is

the soul of our brand', says the company's chief executive, Jean-Marc Gaucher. 'We are not in the fashion world; fashion is chasing the dance world.'[1] He recently launched a project to eliminate as much as possible of the noise caused by the wooden pointes on the floor, and to reduce the pain felt by dancers. 'I have been working with the research department of a university to make these shoes, and now we have reduced the noise by 61 per cent, and professional dancers, and the dancers just under that level, tell us that they don't feel pain in these new shoes.'[2]

After Rose's death, in 1984, the brand fell into the doldrums, but Gaucher, originally a French athlete and a former chief executive of Reebok France, bought the company in 1999. Since then, he has successfully reinstated its wares as part of the modern capsule wardrobe. Collaborations with such labels as Comme des Garçons, Yohji Yamamoto and Rodarte have made Repetto more relevant to high fashion, while the introduction of new styles – lace-up boots and soft leather shoes among them – have expanded the possibilities for consumers. There is also a bespoke service, launched in 2011, in which one is able to choose precisely the shade of leather for a pair of pumps, as well as from a rainbow of options for the grosgrain trimming.

In 2009 a Condé Nast survey announced that Repetto was the favourite luxury shoe brand of 36 per cent of French women; the label now has three shops in its homeland, and in excess of 800 stockists in more than 60 countries across the world. Nearly all its shoes (a few high-heeled exceptions are made elsewhere in Europe) are still produced in the factory at Saint-Médard-d'Excideuil in the rural Dordogne, a town in which the highlight of the calendar is the label's sample sale, when fans come on pilgrimage and queues extend around the block.

An army of celebrity fans has also furthered the brand's fame: Catherine Deneuve, Angelina Jolie, Scarlett Johansson and Sarah Jessica Parker are regulars, while Mick Jagger has also been seen in the label's footwear. Gaucher claims to have received an order from Michael Jackson for a batch of Repetto shoes the day after the singer died, and the brand subsequently launched the Jackson loafer, which sold out in the Paris boutique and was seen on the feet of Kate Moss.

Serge Gainsbourg allegedly wore Repetto's white Zizi lace-ups every day of the year. Rose Repetto created the style for her daughter-in-law Zizi Jeanmarie, and legend has it that Jane Birkin once found a pair on a discount rack and bought them for Gainsbourg, who took to wearing them without socks. They soon became part of his trademark ensemble. 'He wanted shoes that felt like gloves,' Birkin told *Vanity Fair* in 2007, 'so I got him white Repetto ballet shoes.'[3]

1. Quoted in Carola Long, 'Killer Flats: Brigitte Bardot's Secret Style Weapon', *The Independent*, 27 March 2010; independent.co.uk/1926703.html (accessed June 2012).
2. Quoted in *ibid*.
3. Quoted in Lisa Robinson, 'The Secret World of Serge Gainsbourg', *Vanity Fair*, November 2007; vanityfair.com/culture/features/2007/11/gainsbourg200711 (accessed June 2012).

Repetto's shoes originally came in traditional shades suited to the ballerinas who bought them, but they are now available in almost any colour or pattern, and can be bought bespoke, allowing the customer to choose the colour and type of trim.

Robert Clergerie

Opposite Dinato cut-out wedge.

Left Robert Clergerie.

Robert Clergerie's name is synonymous with the boundary-pushing space-age designers who came to maturity during the 1970s in Paris. His structural, often chunky shoes went a step beyond the traditionally French notion of chic, and experimented with form, colour and function in an entirely new way.

But the roots of Clergerie's company go deep. The label as we know it was amalgamated from two footwear brands housed under the umbrella term La Société Romanaise de la Chaussure: Joseph Fenestrier and UNIC. Fenestrier was the son of a tradesman based in Romans-sur-Isère, in the Rhône Valley, still home to the Robert Clergerie business hub and also to the Musée Internationale de la Chaussure, which houses pieces by designers as diverse as Stephane Kélian, Paraboot and Accessoire Diffusion. Fenestrier bought a small shoe factory there in 1895, and became one of the first industrialists to put the town – which had previously been known for its tanneries – on the footwear map. By 1901 he had implemented the Goodyear welt technique (where the inner sole and upper are attached to a piece of leather or plastic before being attached to

Robert Clergerie's was one of the first companies in France to invest in the mass production of footwear.

the sole itself), and his shoes gained a reputation for sturdiness and durability.

Between 1910 and 1916 Fenestrier's company enjoyed unprecedented success, winning awards at several international fairs, including those in Brussels, London, Turin, Ghent and San Francisco. The name had become – to the cognoscenti – a byword for fine men's footwear. By 1926 Fenestrier had consolidated his success into a trading group that consisted of three factories and 800 workers, who produced 1200 pairs of shoes each day. Such a turnover was impressive for the era, when mass production was relatively new. By 1948 a prestigious flagship store was open on the rue du Faubourg Saint-Honoré, Paris, and it flourished in the post-war years under the sartorial instructions of Christian Dior's New Look and during the golden age of Parisian couture, until Fenestrier's death in 1961.

The young Robert Clergerie (born 1934) was then training at the Charles Jourdan Group, which he left in 1978 with the idea of setting up his own label. His first move was to buy the near-defunct Société Romanaise. By 1981 he had established an eponymous women's label, which took its immediate inspiration from the masculine designs the company was producing under its Fenestrier label. Clergerie was among the first to propose classic brogues for female customers, and their simplicity caught on, propelling the company to the upper ranks of fashionable footwear designers and providing the means for more than a decade of expansion.

After retiring in 1996, Clergerie returned to the industry and re-purchased the rights to his name, taking the helm once more in 2004 before installing the designer Roland Mouret,

who created the now-infamous body-hugging Galaxy dress, as creative director in 2011. Clergerie's name has become forever linked, in footwear circles, with simplicity, a concept that is at the heart of his designs. Even if his shoes are futuristic or seemingly complex, they always possess his trademark clarity and purity of aspect: a wooden platform sole topped with Perspex and Velcro-fastening straps; a patent Mary-Jane pump with a thick wedge sole; a typical strapped sandal with an intermediate heel that props up the wearer's foot under its arch and gives a tripartite walking structure. 'In my creations, I always respect the basic principle learned from the famous bootmaker André Perugia', he explains, 'that you carry a garment, but for a shoe, it is different: the shoes carries you, and all the difficulty is here.'[1]

Clergerie's shoes may look challenging to wear, but they are never difficult to walk in; their inherent pragmatism may come across as clunky, but it fits into Clergerie's view of the world. Shoes are made, or discovered rather, in new forms and materials, from a combination of new techniques and artisan habits. Such is the success of the brand that Clergerie himself has been honoured three times by the Fashion Footwear Association of New York with its Designer of the Year prize (in 1987, 1990 and 1992), while in 2005 he was inducted into *Footwear News* magazine's Hall of Fame. Of all the extant footwear brands in France today, Robert Clergerie has most strongly built on its historic roots to drive forwards the design concepts in the field, combining tradition with progress, concept with function, and old with new.

1. Taken from email correspondence between Robert Clergerie and the author, January/February 2012.

Roger Vivier

I f Christian Dior was the master of couture, then his collaborator Roger Vivier (1907–1998) was the father of footwear. Vivier's work in the mid-twentieth century literally changed the shape of shoes forever, with his invention of the platform sole in 1937 and the stiletto in 1954.

Roger Vivier's shoes have been worn by everyone from the Queen (whose coronation shoes flashed with garnets to mimic the scarlet of the Union Jack) to Marlene Dietrich, and the Beatles to Mistinguett, while the man himself has worked with some of the biggest names in fashion, from Dior to Emanuel Ungaro and Yves Saint Laurent. 'He dusted off sketches and gave them the implacability of finished drawings', Saint Laurent said of his long-term friend and colleague.[1]

Vivier was an extravagant and dedicated art collector, working solely in the realms of aesthetics and opulence. But one of his greatest achievements was to provide shoes that went some way towards liberating women. While some might argue that the high heel is a gilded cage, there are plenty who believe that Vivier's transformation of the utilitarian into art – through the development of ingenious heel shapes and shoe structures – was an integral part of ready-to-wear becoming just that, and of making life accessible for women. With the advent of trouser suits and the relaxation of formal dress codes came a freedom that women had not known before, and Vivier's designs were part of it. His shoes were, the company itself says, 'a weapon of fatal attraction for women'.[2]

With that in mind, the cult of the shoe can really be put down to Roger Vivier. Embellishing his designs with such materials as kingfisher feathers, pearls, scales and garlands, he created shoes that were subject to the same intense scrutiny and rigorous design process as a couture gown, and was the first to devote such time to footwear. Little wonder, then, that Christian Dior unveiled his New Look collection with models wearing suitably innovative stilettos created by Vivier. Show shoes were

Opposite Limelight.

Above Roger Vivier in his studio, May 1953.

Below Belle Vivier.

From top Belle Vivier;
Belle de Nuit.

Vivier's job, first and foremost, but he also became the first shoe designer to create a ready-to-wear line in the 1960s.

In 1945 Vivier created a pair of transparent plastic shoes, which seemed at that time to have been summoned from the future. In 1959 he developed the 'shock heel' (so called because of its effect on fashion editors of the time), which curved inwards under the foot. And in 1963 he invented the 'comma heel', which rolled from the heel towards the toes and marked the end of the stiletto's reign as the most popular style. In the same way that Dior reinvented silhouettes with every new season, from the New Look line to the A-line and even the H-line, chopping and changing disparately and efficiently, Vivier reimagined shoes. They were given radical overhauls according to which influences were uppermost in the designer's mind.

Vivier also designed the shoes that matched Yves Saint Laurent's groundbreaking Mondrian collection, shown in Paris in 1965. Incorporating the graphic solidity of the shift dresses on show, themselves inspired by the work of the Dutch De Stijl artist, Vivier's La Belle Vivier pump came with a chunky buckle on the front, a detail that has become a motif of the label.

The brand's current creative director, Bruno Frisoni, who has held the post since 2004, has reintroduced the comma heel in shining steel, and used the buckle as an emblem of the Roger Vivier heritage, on zin leather, rendered in crocodile suede and updated with metallic finishes. 'This emblem of the Vivier spirit seemed the most obvious signature,' he explains, 'especially as it lends itself to so many interpretations. In my view, this isn't a reissue, it's a reinterpretation.'[3]

It has become a calling card, of sorts, for the elegant modernity that Roger Vivier himself embraced. Indeed, La Belle Vivier was seen as such a prop to the modern and empowered woman that it is the style the actress Catherine Deneuve conspicuously slips on in the film *Belle de Jour* (1967) before she embarks on a campaign of infidelity and promiscuity.

Vivier's name accrued further chic credentials with the appointment of the former supermodel Inès de La Fressange to the role of brand ambassador, charged with the task of reviving the label. 'Instead of going out to find a top business school graduate, [Diego Della Valle, the owner of Tod's and Roger Vivier] asked me to revive the label', she told the press. 'It's a bit like Balenciaga. Brands like Vivier are pillars – they are monuments of fashion; they are names we don't forget.'[4]

1. Quoted in material from Roger Vivier press office.
2. Quoted in *ibid*.
3. Quoted in *ibid*.
4. Quoted in interview with Sarah Lerfel, *Interview*, December 2011; interviewmagazine.com/fashion/ines-de-la-fressange (accessed April 2012).

Left (from top) Natalie Portman at the Academy Awards, February 2011; Liv Tyler at a Metropolitan Museum of Art gala, May 2010.

Below Chips ballerina flat.

Rupert Sanderson

I am very moved by the process of making shoes; there is a spareness to mine, where the line is formed by the materials, to create a shoe that is as clean and simple as possible. The best design is the least design, in my opinion. Less is more.'[1] So says Rupert Sanderson (born 1966), shoemaker to socialites and a reformed advertising executive who dropped out of the rat-race to study at Cordwainers in London. So much is obvious in the way he sees his pieces not as art or sculpture but as products. There is much that is eminently practical and pragmatic at the heart of his aesthetic, born perhaps of an awareness of – not to mention a grounding in – giving customers what they want.

'It's an old-fashioned way to treat a shoe,' Sanderson continues, 'but they are not a vehicle for the avant-garde or for self-expression. They are a recognized item of fashion that is not dictated to by fashion. I always try to create something new, but something that retains a certain handwriting.'

That 'handwriting' is seen in plain and unembellished designs that take shape from a focus on the curves and sensuality of the lasts from which they are made, and the heels that balance them. These are shoes designed with the aim of flattering their wearer, not of distracting or detracting from them by making any more of a statement than the simple fact that they are being worn.

'It's unfashionable, but, as [the industrial designer] Dieter Rams said, I believe in good design', explains Sanderson. 'I take a modernist approach – but it's more "don't scare the horses". When you burst on to the scene, you risk being defined by the initial thing you did. But for a shoemaker, the design must be graceful. It's not about fireworks, it's to do with longevity.'

The sense of the modern classic is obvious from such shoes as Sanderson's Malone courts, or the pointed-toe Vista. The former has a 4-inch (10-cm) heel and is made from kid leather with a rounded toe and square instep; the latter has a 3-inch (8-cm) heel and is made from patent leather, with an asymmetrical topline. Such sturdy, comfortable, daywear-cum-eveningwear shoes as these

The London-based designer Rupert Sanderson left a career in advertising to train at Cordwainers. Such models as Meledor (opposite) and Laira (below) are emblematic of his modern and practical view of classically feminine footwear.

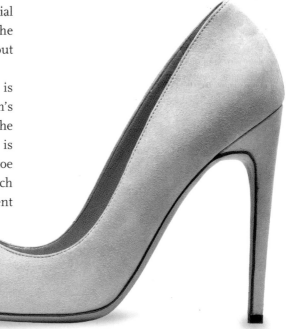

Sanderson's style is elegant, classic and feminine, and his aim to give everyday comfort a more glamorous (and less practical) edge, earning him a legion of fans and customers. Pictured clockwise from right are Lintie; Nissa; Kitkat; Kibo.

have made Rupert Sanderson a name to rely on among the cognoscenti, and his rose-gold logo is now a sign of being in the know. And that is understood not only by celebrity fans, such as the Duchess of Cambridge and Gwyneth Paltrow, but also by the businesswomen and creative people who wear his shoes, from art historians to fashion buyers – some of whom choose to feature on Sanderson's website, in the role of guest editor for a brand they have come to love.

'I shy away from the term "classics"', Sanderson explains. 'Shoes that are new that season are by definition not "classics". An extremely complex shoe can become a classic, because it can define an era. The timelessness I try to achieve is part of good design, not necessarily "classic" but simply "of itself". You're dead in the water if you never change; fashion is inevitably moving forwards – it's a fast-running stream to work in.'

But for all that Sanderson is fully part of the British fashion industry (he writes a regular blog for British *Vogue* in his spare time), he has proved his mettle by working beyond that stream, too. Having trained at Sergio Rossi and Bruno Magli, Sanderson spent a summer holiday while he was at Cordwainers travelling between Italian factories on his motorbike, to speak to suppliers, before founding his own label in 2001. In 2006 he bought a controlling stake in the Italian factory that produces his shoes, in order that he might safeguard precisely the techniques and hallmarks of his signature style.

Sanderson has created footwear for Karl Lagerfeld's eponymous label (p. 153), and has worked with such young British designers

From top A cut-out sandal; Piccadilly.

Sanderson trained at Sergio Rossi and Bruno Magli, and continues a tradition of almost couture-like attention to detail in footwear. Clockwise from right: a shoe designed by Rupert Sanderson for the Osman Spring/Summer 2012 catwalk show; Devon pony-skin; Asteroid (Robert Sanderson for Karl Lagerfeld, Spring/Summer 2010); Gold Amneris for *Aida* (2010); ankle-strap stiletto.

Rupert Sanderson indulges in whimsical touches, and his famously imaginative approach has led to numerous collaborations. Pictured on this page are (clockwise from right) Estelle; python boot; Troy.

as Osman Yousefzada and Louise Goldin. In 2010 he created shoes for the entire cast of David McVicar's production of Verdi's *Aida* at the Royal Opera House, Covent Garden. 'I had a [long] lead time of eighteen months, which is unheard of in the fashion world', he says of the brief, for which he produced beautifully intricate gold platform sandals that featured within their soles a carved rendering of a prostrate figure (p. 152, bottom right). 'It was a relief to be part of a team for once, and to be subjugated to the production. It's not like the catwalk, you don't have to woo buyers with your ideas.'

Not that Sanderson dilutes his ideas for the market; it is more that he knows what his own market is keen to wear. 'You don't get points for practicality. People are not interested in comfort in a shoe. I don't make comfy shoes, but I do respect the fact that they are shoes. I will always compete on pure design', he says proudly. 'There's no fancy branding here.'

1. All quotations from Rupert Sanderson are taken from a telephone conversation with the author, January 2012.

Chanel

When Gabrielle 'Coco' Chanel (1883–1971; pictured above, left, in 1969) began designing clothes, she fought against established codes of female dress that she believed were restrictive and which prevented women from living as full a life as men. She broke down the formality of clothing in the early twentieth century, loosening waists, shortening skirts and jettisoning the rigid underpinnings of corsets and girdles.

With this process, naturally, came a review of footwear. Chanel's shoes, which she launched more than fifty years ago, were based on the same premise as her clothing. Low-heeled courts came in two-tone cream and black, just like her monochrome shift dresses and separates, with a simple bow fastening at the front and plain, rounded toes.

In 1957 came the Chanel ballet pump, which has since entered the canon, and is partially responsible for the rehabilitation of the ballet pump as an everyday shoe. Chanel gave it a beige leather upper chassis and topped it off with a black leather toecap, inspired (it is said) by men's brogues, to make these dainty shoes more durable. The toecaps were embossed with the label's interlinking 'C' logo.

These pumps are still for sale now, as are handbags designed by Chanel herself; they are not the sort of style that ever goes out of fashion. But their personality and target customer have been reassigned in recent years. Having been a wardrobe staple for the bourgeoisie, these *bon chic, bon genre* stalwarts were picked up in the mid-2000s by such stars as the British model and television presenter Alexa Chung, who breathed new life and a sense of streetwear into them.

It was around this time that Chanel's creative director, Karl Lagerfeld, became more interested in the possibilities of footwear within the brand, and his collections since have expanded greatly and become influential in the field. At a film premiere in 2008, the singer Madonna wore a pair of Chanel's Miami Vice platforms from Spring/Summer 2009, with a heel shaped like a classic revolver (above, right). The design instantly caused controversy, with anti-gun protesters describing it as glamorizing violence and crime. In the catwalk show, these shoes had been made with real gun casings; the retail versions were replaced with a 3½-inch-long (9 cm) Perspex rendering.

For Spring/Summer 2010 Lagerfeld staged a show that resembled an enormous barn dance, with models wearing slip-on clogs with thick wooden soles. It was the first time such a shoe had been on a high-end catwalk since the 1970s at least, and it had never before been shown in so naively pastoral a version. Lagerfeld's came in leather and fabric, in shades of pearl and black, decorated with corsages and clusters of faux-rustic woven poppies.

Lagerfeld has continued his vision in shoes for Autumn/Winter 2010–11 he showed thigh-high faux-fur yeti boots, and for Spring/Summer 2012, shoes took inspiration from his 'under the sea' theme, with heels made to look like shards of coral. At the label's Autumn/Winter 2012–13 show, models wore asymmetrical shoes that resembled T-bar court shoes from one side and ankle boots from the other

Salvatore Ferragamo

Opposite This design was probably created for a famous client, possibly Judy Garland. It is in the collection of the Metropolitan Museum of Art, New York.

Left Pietro Annigoni (1910–1988), *Salvatore Ferragamo*, 1949, oil on canvas.

Below *Oggi* magazine, May 1960. Contemporary articles referred to Ferragamo as Italy's top footwear designer.

After more than eighty years in business, the house of Ferragamo has come a long way from its origins as a Florentine shoemaker. Nowadays the label is synonymous with Italian luxury and fashion, with a women's ready-to-wear clothing collection released four times a year, as well as high-end accessories, including luggage, fragrance and scarves, which sit alongside the footwear that made the name one of the most famous in shoe design.

But the history of the label actually begins even earlier, at the beginning of the twentieth century, when the founder, Salvatore Ferragamo, left his Italian village and travelled to Hollywood, where he began fitting starlets for shoes. The eleventh of fourteen children, Ferragamo was born near Naples in 1898 and made his first pair of shoes at the age of nine. His first contract was with the American Film Company, which ordered a job lot of cowboy boots for westerns; Ferragamo created jingling spurs for Rudolph Valentino and Douglas Fairbanks, among others. But it was only on his return to Italy in 1927 and the founding of his Florence shop in 1928 that his name became a brand.

Right Invisible sandal, 1949. This shoe was described as 'revolutionary' when it first appeared.

Far right Salvatore Ferragamo moved his workshop to Palazzo Spini Feroni, Florence, in 1936, and bought the palazzo two years later.

Right, bottom The iconic Vara shoe is a block-heeled pump that made the Italian label famous across the globe. Designed by Ferragamo's daughter Fiamma in 1978, it is still sold today.

Throughout the golden age of cinema, Ferragamo continued to make shoes for such stars as Greta Garbo, Audrey Hepburn and Marilyn Monroe. Working through the leather shortages of the Second World War, he became known for his ingenuity and innovation, improvising with such materials as cork or cellophane. Through his pioneering use of such alternatives, the now-ubiquitous cork wedge was born, as was the 'invisible sandal' (left, top, and p. 162, top), a style that made use of a nylon upper so that the foot supports were barely seen.

After the war, the company's head-quarters at the medieval Palazzo Spini Feroni in Florence (above) became a site of pilgrimage for the rich and famous, who travelled there to attend fittings and place personal orders. There remain in the company's archives the lasts made by Ferragamo himself from impressions of the feet of such stars as Lauren Bacall and

From top Iride court shoe, 1935–36; Kimo sandal, 1951; Sandal, 1942–44.

Sophia Loren; Ferragamo never destroyed a last once it had been created, so that the client could forever have shoes made perfectly to measure by the company.

The celebrities kept coming until Ferragamo's death in 1960, when the helm of the company was taken by his wife and children and the brand expanded its product range and production methods to become international. Today there are more than 520 Salvatore Ferragamo stores worldwide, and in 2009 the firm recorded a turnover of more than €620 million. The year 1995 saw the opening of a museum in Florence dedicated to the brand, the insignia of which remains the handwritten signature of the man who founded it.

The footwear that continues to sell retains Ferragamo's expression, too: the iconic Vara (p. 158, bottom left), a block-heeled court shoe created by his daughter Fiamma in 1978, comes in almost any colour (another signature of Ferragamo shoes is the vast assortment of shades available), and the Varina, a reworked ballet-pump update of the cult classic, still features the grosgrain ribbon and metal buckle front-piece. 'When it came out, the boutique line didn't have a model that was both sporty and elegant', Fiamma explained in an interview. 'The designers set to work on a style that had been tried and tested for some seasons and was well known to be comfortable, with a low heel and a round toe.'

Such are the essential practicality and ease of the Varina that it has become one of the brand's bestselling items, with cohorts of fans buying pairs in various colours. Its timeless modesty has earned it admirers around the world, and Ferragamo has an

Ferragamo shoes are characterized by great brightness and vibrancy; they were originally made for some of the most creative people of Hollywood's golden age. Illustrated on these pages are campaign images from Spring/Summer 1997 (opposite), Autumn/Winter 2011–12 (above, with the model Daria Werbowy) and Spring/Summer 2012 (left, with Gisele Bündchen).

Right Invisible sandal, 1947. The idea of using fishing line for the upper came to Ferragamo as he leaned out of a window in Palazzo Spini Feroni and watched fishermen on the River Arno.

Below Pull-over, 1930. The sandal came back into fashion in the 1920s and '30s, after the Victorian period, when it had been considered unseemly for women to expose their feet.

almost legendary status in such countries as Japan and the United Arab Emirates, where leading figures are regularly seen wearing the label's designs.

During the 1980s Ferragamo leather pumps became a status symbol as part of the 'power dressing' code adopted by women intent on making their mark in the realm of business. Together with suits in masculine cuts and high-necked blouses, as well as high-end silk scarves and gold jewellery, Ferragamo pumps were part of the wardrobe of women who wanted to be seen as hard-headed but not hard-hearted. The breadth of design within the range was almost certainly part of its appeal. But the essence of the Vara court was its sturdiness and reliability, paired with feminine adornment – chic, but not over-embellished.

Salvatore Ferragamo is one of fashion's great success stories. He may have started out as 'shoemaker to the stars', as his native Italian media dubbed him on his return from California, but his name endures as a shoemaker to just about everybody else, too. It is a suitably democratic end for a man whose aim was comfort and fit, along with imagination and wit, and just a hint of old-school glamour.

Shoes from Ferragamo have always had a backstory in terms of inspiration. Here, archive advertising designed by Lucio Venna in 1930 explains the origin of three models.

Swedish Hasbeens

With the proliferation of Scandinavian labels in the early years of the twenty-first century came a more thorough investigation of the region's style credentials in general. One element of traditional Swedish garb, the wooden-soled clog, underwent a high-fashion transformation for Spring/Summer 2010, when Karl Lagerfeld experimented with platform versions for his Chanel collection, and they also cropped up on the catwalk at Chloé, among several other labels. The Stockholm-based brand Swedish Hasbeens looks to this heritage with its wooden-soled collections, developing the clog aesthetic from the original 1970s-style leather strapped upper with a solid wooden sole into more modern and innovative styles, such as Chelsea boots, lace-ups and loafers.

Wooden footwear has its roots in classical antiquity, in the 'buskin', a high, thick-soled boot worn by the members of the chorus in Greek tragedies, and the 'caliga' shoe worn by Roman soldiers. It is likely, too, that the Jutes and Saxons were familiar with wooden footwear – or, at least, wooden-soled footwear – given that wood

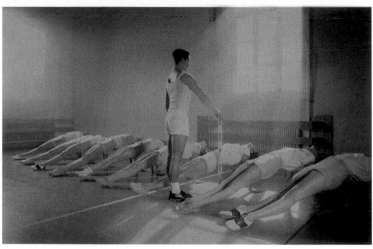

Distinctive yet archetypal, toffels by Swedish Hasbeens (opposite) identify wryly with some of the stereotypes associated with their homeland in campaigns and images that set out to mock and provoke (left, top and bottom).

Right The traditional clog has a wooden sole and leather uppers, but Swedish Hasbeens has reworked the aesthetic – and the materials – into a diverse range of shoes, from boots to high heels and brogues.

Opposite Recent advertising campaigns have emphasized the brand's retro appeal.

was one of the most easily obtained and durable materials available to them.

Traditional Dutch and French clogs are made entirely from wood and are intended as an overshoe or protective layer during outdoor work, and for ceremonial use. Swedish clogs or 'toffels', however, the basis for all Swedish Hasbeens collections, and English clogs are more recognizably similar to the modern clog, with wooden soles and leather uppers, riveted with large nails and given plastic sole coverings to prevent the wood from wearing down. Clogs were primarily worn in Britain during the Industrial Revolution of the nineteenth century, but in Sweden they are still considered to be everyday footwear. Indeed, as Swedish Hasbeens has proved, they are downright fashionable.

Founded in 2006 by Swedes Emy Blixt and Cilla Wingård Neuman, Swedish Hasbeens was born from the discovery of a warehouse full of 300 pairs of original 1970s toffels, slated to be destroyed. So redolent were they of the founders' mothers, and of a particularly Swedish-influenced 1970s aesthetic, that Blixt and Neuman decided to try to sell them. They were an instant hit, and Hasbeens are now sold in more than twenty countries, with the impressive claim that it was Swedish toffels that finally separated Sarah Jessica Parker on the set of the *Sex and the City* film from her Choos and her Manolos.

As well as having fashion credentials – the season the clog was rehabilitated saw the emergence of another trend, dubbed by the style press 'the Seventies mum', into which Hasbeens fed rather well – the brand is part of a growing movement towards ethically

made, naturally sourced goods produced on a small scale. After the initial consignment of vintage models had been distributed, the founders of Swedish Hasbeens developed links to small factories and artisans working in the traditional way. Every pair of toffels, be they the classic sandals or heeled boots, is made by hand from tanned leather, and lime and alder wood, cut from one piece rather than amalgamated from composite parts. This is crucial in a wooden-soled shoe, where joins would increase the risk of water damage and warping.

The development of the traditional form into modern and trend-influenced styles is also interesting, as it works on the assumption that wood is suited to footwear more generally, rather than simply a specific model. From the platform soles of the heeled sandals or high-heeled Jodhpur boots to the much thinner, flat soles of the

A simple palette and
nostalgic styling give
Swedish Hasbeens a
naive, vintage feel.

ballerina Hepburn variety, the way wood is used has been calibrated as part of the production process. This marks Swedish Hasbeens as a label working in an essentially new vein: the reinterpretation of traditional methods for modern, renewable purposes.

As cult shoes go, Hasbeens are relatively new, but their practicality, comfort and environmental credentials cement their position as a brand to look out for. They are already a recognizable presence in magazines and shops, making more impact as functional streetwear than as directional editorial items, perhaps. But that is how a shoe attains cult status: by being worn. There is something naive and youthful about the bright colours – toffels come in red, green, blue, yellow, buttery tan (or 'nature'), white and black – but the shoes also project a sense of timelessness that means they exist above and beyond any usual trend in footwear.

'Our style is very basic and down-to-earth, yet innovative and daring', says Blixt. 'We are very creative without drawing exaggerated attention – and we get a lot of attention because of that. It's a contradiction, in a way, but a really great one.'[1]

1. Taken from email correspondence between Emy Blixt and the author, January/February 2012.

Terry de Havilland

High heels have to be worn with confidence and plenty of attitude', says Terry de Havilland. 'In this way, they become empowering.'[1] The celebrity fans of De Havilland's eponymous label certainly have both attributes in spades, boasting not only Kate Moss and Sienna Miller among their number, but also such superstars as Cher, David Bowie, Michelle Pfeiffer and Jackie Onassis. De Havilland created platforms for the actor Tim Curry's role in *The Rocky Horror Picture Show* (1975), and made more than thirty pairs of desert boots for Angelina Jolie to wear in the *Tomb Raider* films. The dancer Rudolf Nureyev forsook his usual ballet pumps for a pair of knee-high python boots by De Havilland, and the singer Kylie Minogue has worn his shoes on stage in many of her tours.

'If I had to cite an inspiration, it would be music,' De Havilland explains, 'all manner of music and street style. I do love a rock chick and I do love working to a brief when it comes to costume and stagewear.' His pieces are undoubtedly theatrical, both in size and in scope: made from sinuous skins in soaring architectural shapes, aggressively unwieldy-looking and yet

De Havilland's footwear has attained cult status not only by being worn onstage by the likes of David Bowie, but also for its finesse and elegance, and through the wit and irreverance of its maker, a veritable 'shoe-turier'. The shoe pictured opposite is Luna; the model (left) wears Mandi.

De Havilland's design signatures are inspired by yesteryear, with block heels and chunky platforms that refer to 1930s-era glamour via 1970s glam rock. Pictured on this page are (from top) Carina; Nicole Alba; Angelina.

unexpectedly light. His stacked cyber-goth Transmuter boots became a cult classic in the late 1990s after the rock star Marilyn Manson added them to his collection, but De Havilland had been dressing icons of the music industry for a long time by then.

Terry de Havilland (born 1938) began his career as a shoe designer at the age of five, in his parents' footwear company, Waverley Shoes. He cut his first pair in 1957 while on leave from National Service, and designed his first bestsellers for the family firm in 1960. By 1964 his pieces were being featured in the style press, and in 1969 he designed the three-tiered coloured wedges for which he has become so well known, earning the patronage of Bianca Jagger and Bette Midler. That was the beginning of a label that would go from strength to strength for more than fifty years.

Commercial interest has understandably ebbed and flowed with trends, but De Havilland is known as the master of the discotheque shoe, his idiosyncratic designs inhabiting a space between diva and drag, glitterball and grunge. His name is synonymous with a certain kind of glamour that is never unfashionable for long. There are two types of shoe in his œuvre, he explains: fierce and gorgeous. The melding of the two is where he finds his own unique strength.

'I'm a bit of a maverick', De Havilland says. 'When I reintroduced platform wedges, it was totally instinctive.' In 2003 he was enlisted by the stylist Karl Plewka to create the footwear for the actress Sadie Frost's FrostFrench catwalk show, and he decided to array models in his most iconic style. 'They were totally off-trend, but within the space of twelve months, the wedge began to appear everywhere.'

De Havilland designs straight on to the last, a technique that allows him to shape the shoe more diligently with the wearer's comfort in mind. He creates prototypes himself so that his wife, Liz, is able to try them on. His signature disco wedges are fitted with what he calls 'springolators', elastic struts within the straps that allow the shoes to cling more readily to the foot, lessening the need for toe-clenching or foot-flexing to keep them on. 'There's nothing worse than seeing a woman struggling painfully in a pair of too-high heels', he says. 'It's the antithesis of sexy.'

After the death of his father, De Havilland (then known as Terence Higgins) took over the family business and opened his first shop, Cobblers to the World, on the King's Road, Chelsea, in 1972. After that came Kamikaze Shoes in the 1980s. Neither venture remained open in the long term, but De Havilland's shoes have gone the distance, encapsulating at once an heirloom quality and a timelessness with every generation that discovers them afresh. He describes his footwear as 'retro future classics', a synopsis of their 1930s-meets-1970s-meets-science-fiction aesthetic.

'I'm probably best known for my metallic multicoloured platforms and wedges,' De Havilland agrees, 'but there is another side to my work that is very attitudinal and comic book-inspired.' Dagger is an ankle boot with a silver dagger in place of a heel, and Dragon a silk-screen-printed red-and-gold wedge, while Leyla is an emerald lace mule. There are also latex thigh boots and commando-soled flats, the latter

From top Charlie; Jay; Mindy.

Often rendered in bright colours or with characteristic eccentricity, De Havilland's shoes are not for shrinking violets. Clockwise from right: Mandi; Lisette; Emma; Zia.

developed initially for his wife after a back injury, and now worn on stage by the singer Jessie J (right, centre).

De Havilland found his pseudonym one evening in Rome at a party above the Trevi Fountain, in which Federico Fellini was filming Anita Ekberg in *La Dolce Vita* (1960). The moniker prompted Cher to believe that De Havilland was 'gay, French and dead', but the designer describes his sensibilities as uniquely English. 'My father made shoes for the Windmill Girls during the war', he says. 'Platforms and ankle straps are in my psyche.'[2]

1. All quotations from Terry de Havilland are taken from email correspondence with the author, December 2011–February 2012.
2. Hannah Betts, interview with Terry de Havilland, *The Telegraph*, 11 July 2011.

Above De Havilland's shoes represent concepts and themes realized for the wearer. His celebrity clientele includes many musicians, because his pieces conform so perfectly to stage criteria in their sturdy boldness. Pictured here are (left to right) Amy Winehouse at the Coachella Valley Music and Arts Festival, April 2007; Jessie J at T4 Stars of 2011, London, December 2011; Beth Ditto at the Brit Awards, February 2008.

Left Luna and Margaux.

Tod's

From a shoemaking business that opened in the 1940s with one employee, the Italian label Tod's has become an international footwear superpower. It now employs more than 3000 people worldwide, with outposts in Dubai, New York, London and Tokyo, to name but a few; assets of more than €915 million at the end of 2010; and sales in excess of $450 million. It is also the parent company of in-house labels Hogan and Fay, and acquired the French footwear label Roger Vivier (pp. 145–47) in the mid-1990s.

It began with Dorino Della Valle, whose son Diego is now chief executive of the company. Dorino's basement workshop ran a brisk trade in Casette d'Ete in the Marche region of Italy, where many of his descendants still live, and supplied shoes to such labels as Calvin Klein and Azzedine Alaïa. Dorino's father, Filippo, was also a cobbler, and his workbench still takes pride of place on the second floor of the factory. But his son and grandsons began to expand the workshop's output in the 1970s, and turned it into a factory that supplied American department stores with high-quality shoes made from sought-after Italian leather.

Opposite Tod's iconic Gommino driving shoe has become one of the most bankable, bestselling shoes in the world.

Above, left Limited-edition Gommini in embroidered suede.

Above Diego Della Valle, Tod's chief executive.

Left The Tod's store at Via della Spiga 22, Milan.

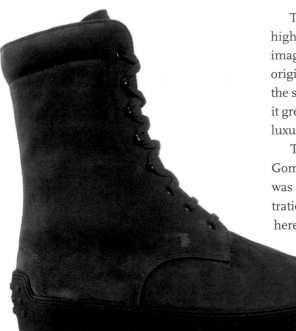

Diego Della Valle's creation of a cult classic and entire company is a footwear fairytale. The name Tod's was chosen from a Boston telephone directory.

The success of Tod's is born not only of high quality but also of innovation and imaginative marketing. Using its artisanal origins and the tradesman's knowledge of the small shoemaking business from which it grew, Tod's has become a globally minded luxury titan.

The development of the signature Gommino loafer (p. 176) in the late 1970s was a masterstroke of commercial concentration that ensured the brand's ubiquity: here was comfort and chic in a traditional, hand-sewn style that worked for everyday and had a hefty dose of the preppy aesthetic beloved of the upper echelons of American society. Each slipper requires about 120 different stages of assembly, and each pair is cut from a single hide to ensure a consistency of grain, and is made up of more than seventy pieces. Lasts are hand-carved on the premises by a modellist, and each shoe is assembled by hand from a selection of hides that includes calfskin, gazelle, anaconda, ostrich and crocodile – in quantities of up to 20 million square feet at any given moment.

The name 'Gommino' ('little pebbles') derives from the style's soles, which are studded with precisely 133 rubber nodules that distribute weight and pressure evenly across the sole of the foot, give grip and stability, and make walking easier. Even better, the style is essentially unisex, bar minor adjustments.

'At the time everything was very precise: black suit, blue shirt and tie', Diego Della Valle told *Time* magazine in 2006. 'There was nothing casual. For me, it was very important to find something light, to combine good taste with free time.'[1] The rubber-soled driving shoe was born, and the company took its name from a listing in a Boston telephone directory, to give it that all-American sense of homogeneity.

Over the years the Gommino has accrued legions of fans, from such celebrities as Sarah Jessica Parker and Gwyneth Paltrow (who has fronted the company's advertising campaigns in recent years) to a second wave of buyers in Asia, who turned to the style in the 1990s, when the American look of luxury became an aspirational trend among consumers in Japan, Singapore and Hong Kong. Not only do the practicality and unassuming modesty of the style go down a treat in these countries, but also the 'Made in Italy' label on all Tod's products – which are made in a factory behind the brand's imposing glass headquarters on Strada Brancadoro in Sant'Elpidio a Mare in Fermo, central Italy – has become a status symbol in itself in these markets.

The Fermo region is home to about 90 per cent of Italy's shoe manufacturers, and Diego Della Valle lives near his factory in a seventeenth-century villa. He runs the company with his brother, Andrea, and they have known many of the production managers at the factory since childhood. But the expansion of the company has brought some changes: the brothers are now celebrities themselves, sometimes sparring with former Italian prime minister Silvio Berlusconi, sometimes socializing with a group of friends that includes Ferrari chief executive Luca Cordero di Montezemolo, but always intent on the success of the football club they own, Fiorentina.

And Tod's has gone from strength to strength, developing a luggage range in 1997 that brought the pragmatic principles of its signature shoe into the realm of handbags and accessories. Art collaborations on shoes and in stores, with the likes of production designer Dante Ferretti and illustrator Michael Roberts, jostle for attention with such creative initiatives as the commissioning of Chanel designer Karl Lagerfeld to create a capsule collection of footwear and bags for Tod's second label, Hogan. That brief is altogether more sporty in its remit, focusing as it does on citified, urban trainers rather than upmarket leather goods.

1. Quoted in Kay Betts, 'Driving Force: Diego Della Valle', *Time*, 8 March 2006.

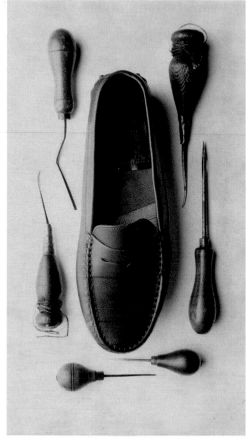

Above The iconic driving shoe during the manufacturing process.

Left Studded soles give Tod's shoes a sense of distinction. The name Gommino, given to the classic slip-on, refers to the rubber sole's 133 nodules, which distribute weight evenly for maximum comfort.

UGG

The rise in popularity of the Australian 'UGG boot' is something of a latterday parable: an obscure trend driven by celebrity endorsement and conspicuous consumption.

UGG boots were first seen in Britain and the United States on the feet of such stars as Kate Moss and Pamela Anderson, who knew the style essentially as a slipper. It was their decision to wear UGGs with jeans, even with sportswear – along with many other famous faces, who plumped for UGG boots as a comfortable option in which to pick up their children from school or do the weekly shop – that made the consuming public aware of the brand.

The sheepskin-lined suede booties originate in Australian surfing practice: they were engineered to be put on after surfing to keep the legs warm. This developed into a more generic use as indoor shoes or loungewear, before the celebrity craze kicked in.

Such origins have led to difficulties with licensing and brand patrolling. The battle over who invented the UGG boot still rages, but the fact that it is known by a brand name would suggest some sort of resolution. This brand name in fact derives

Love it or loathe it, the UGG sheepskin bootie has entered the annals of footwear history for its ubiquity as both a fashion statement and a social compass. Pictured on these pages are the classic tall bomber (opposite); sheepskin cuff boot (left); Ansley shoe with sheepskin lining (left, bottom).

Since the fleece-lined boot became popular in the 2000s, several companies have claimed to be the original purveyor, but UGG was one of the first to capture the audience and diversify its colours, styles and textures. From top: Bailey Button; Classic short boot.

from the word 'ugly'; UGG boots have never billed themselves as a sleek option.

But UGG Australia calls itself the 'official' maker of UGG boots, descended from the handmade 'footies' of surfers in Byron Bay (although similar sheepskin boots were worn in rural New Zealand as early as the 1920s). And it was the UGG variant that made it to the hungry markets in Britain and America in the mid-2000s.

The clamour for UGGs was at first derided, but such derision subsided when the critics realized exactly how comfortable the boots were. There was moral panic, as many claimed the boots had precipitated a 'slob-couture' apocalypse. Indeed, there is a youth subculture of the UGG look that involves teaming a pair with pyjama bottoms. Decriers called the boots ungainly, unflattering, even common; a famous advertising campaign for *The Times* asked if the women who wore them weren't in fact sheep themselves, casting a *Times* reader as the one woman who was not in UGGs. '[They] can instantly transform the prettiest woman in the ... clingiest jeans into a clomping elephant', complained the *Daily Mail* in 2007.[1] And 'knock-off versions of the designer boots are crippling a generation of young women', the paper claimed three years later, 'literally breaking their feet.'[2]

For the main part, however, UGG boots were worn with skinny jeans as part of an increasingly popular 'boho' look promulgated by the likes of Kate Moss and Sienna Miller on the pavements of north London. There were UGGs, too, on the feet of an aspirational clique of footballers' wives, who were also rising to sartorial prominence. The point of an UGG boot was to counter

From top Bellvue; Over-knee Bailey Button.

Right Ronnie Wood at RTÉ Studios, Dublin, October 2010; Hilary Swank filming in New York, March 2011.

Below Adirondack.

some of the hyperbolic glamour demanded by the paparazzi culture of the day; those who wore them were cool for not caring – although the rise of the trend swiftly made that a contradiction in terms.

A sturdy rubber sole supports a calf-high suede upper, seamed at the sides and lined with sheepskin. Many styles feature a sheepskin revers as decorative trim on the exterior of the boot, too. Traditionally made in a tan colour, the boots began to be supplied in pale beige, black and even pink, to cope with demand. The company also branched out into accessories – bags, purses, even ear muffs – all made from the signature suede and sheepskin.

The brand's commercial success has not abated; whether or not the celebrities continue to wear the boots as proudly as they used to, they are still photographed in them, and UGG Australia has become one of the most powerful fashion brands in the world, advertising in most glossy magazines on the racks.

The company has, however, recently decided on a different tack: in 2011 a newly

launched 'UGG Collection', stocked at the luxury boutique Harvey Nichols, aimed to divert attention away from the classic bootie towards a new direction for the label. The range brought some of the brand's trademarks – sheepskin, rubber 'lug' soles, suede and tweed – into a design sphere more readily associated with high fashion, using them to adorn stilettos and court shoes, wedges, biker boots and high-end luggage.

UGG Australia is in this way a company created from a cult shoe, with a market strength and presence dependent on that specific moment of consumer coherence when its products were all anyone wanted. And, to all intents and purposes, that continues to be the case.

1. Vincent Graff, 'The UGGly Truth: They're Hot, Smelly and Bad for Your Feet So Why Are UGG Boots So Popular?', *Daily Mail*, 29 November 2007; dailymail.co.uk/femail/article-497170 (accessed June 2012).
2. Kate Loveys, 'How Cheap Imitation UGG Boots Are "Crippling" a Generation of Fashion Victim Women', *Daily Mail*, 16 March 2010; dailymail.co.uk/femail/article-1258073 (accessed June 2012).

Further Reading

Museums and Collections

Rachelle Bergstein, *Women from the Ankle Down: The Story of Shoes and How They Define Us*, New York (HarperCollins) 2012

Manolo Blahnik and Suzy Menkes, *Manolo's New Shoes*, London and New York (Thames & Hudson) 2010

Tamsin Blanchard, *The Shoe: Best Foot Forward*, London (Carlton Books) 2000

Design Museum, *Fifty Shoes That Changed the World*, London (Conran Octopus) 2009

Sue Huey and Rebecca Proctor, *New Shoes: Contemporary Footwear Design*, London (Laurence King) 2007

Christian Louboutin *et al.*, *Christian Louboutin*, New York (Rizzoli) 2011

Giorgio Riello and Peter McNeil, *Shoes: A History from Sandals to Sneakers*, Oxford and New York (Berg) 2006

Jonathan Walford, *Shoes A–Z: Designers, Brands, Manufacturers and Retailers*, London and New York (Thames & Hudson) 2010

United Kingdom

Design Museum
28 Shad Thames, London SE1 2YD
designmuseum.org

Fashion Museum
Assembly Rooms, Bennett Street,
Bath BA1 2QH
museumofcostume.co.uk

Life and Sole Gallery, Northampton Museum and Art Gallery
Guildhall Road, Northampton NN1 1DP
northampton.gov.uk/museums

Shoe Museum
Clarks headquarters, 40 High Street, Street,
Somerset BA16 0EE

Shoe Museum, Lamberts Mill
Fallbarn Road, off Bocholt Way, Rawtenstall,
Lancashire BB4 7NX
lambertsmill.com/museum.html

Victoria and Albert Museum
Cromwell Road, London SW7 2RL
vam.ac.uk

North America

The Bata Shoe Museum
327 Bloor Street West, Toronto M5S 1W7
batashoemuseum.ca

The Metropolitan Museum of Art
1000 Fifth Avenue, New York, NY 10028-0198
metmuseum.org

The TUSPM Shoe Museum
6th Floor, Temple University School of Podiatric Medicine, 8th and Race Streets,
Philadelphia, PA 19107
podiatry.temple.edu/pages/about/
shoe_museum/shoe_museum.html

Europe

German Leather Museum and Shoe Museum
Frankfurter Strasse 86, D-63067 Offenbach,
Germany
ledermuseum.de

**Musée Internationale de la Chaussure
(International Shoe Museum)**
2 rue Ste-Marie, F-26100 Romans-sur-Isère,
France

Museo Calzado (Footwear Museum)
Avenida de Chapí 32, 03600 Elda
(Alicante-Alacant), Spain
museocalzado.com

Museo della Calzatura (Footwear Museum)
Corso Baccio 35, 63019 Sant'Elpidio a Mare, Italy

Museo Gucci
Piazza della Signoria, Florence, Italy
guccimuseo.com

**Museo Internationale della Calzatura Pietro
Bertolini (Pietro Bertolini International Shoe
Museum)**
Palazzo Crespi, Corso Cavour 82,
27029 Vigevano, Italy

Museo Salvatore Ferragamo
Piazza Santa Trinita 5, 50123 Florence, Italy
museoferragamo.it

**Nationaal Schoeiselmuseum (National
Footwear Museum)**
Wijngaardstraat 9, 8870 Izegem, Belgium
musea.izegem.be/ned/schoeiselmuseum.asp

Shoe Museum
Plaça Sant Felip Neri 5, Barrí Gòtic,
Barcelona, Spain

**Shoe Museum, Muzeum Jihovýchodní
Moravy ve Zlíne**
Soudní 1, 762 57 Zlín, Czech Republic
muzeum-zlin.cz/cs/objekty/obuvnicke-
muzeum

SONS (Shoes or No Shoes?)
Vandevoordeweg 2, 9770 Kruishoutem,
Belgium
shoesornoshoes.com

Vienna Shoe Museum
Florianigasse 66, A-1080 Vienna, Austria
schuhmuseum.at

Asia

Japan Footwear Museum
4-16-27 Matsunagacho, Fukuyama City,
Hiroshima Prefecture 729-0104, Japan
fukuyama-kanko.com/english/hyaka/
cat_spot017.html (in English)
footandtoy.jp (in Japanese)

Marikina Shoe Museum
J.P. Rizal Street, San Roque, Marikina 1800,
The Philippines

Online
virtualshoemuseum.com

Index

Bold page numbers indicate main references; numbers in *italic* refer to the illustrations and their captions

Acknowledgements

This book was written with a broken leg and battered spirits. Thanks to those who watched me mend and helped me to walk again: my parents, for their patience and support; my sisters, for listening; my friends, for keeping me company and keeping me sane. Thanks to the team at Merrell for all their hard work, and to all the designers who have supplied images of their wondrous creations.

Picture credits

Jacket, front Paloma shoe
by Charlotte Olympia; see
pp. 37–41.

Jacket, back Vara shoe by
Salvatore Ferragamo,
Spring/Summer 1997; see
pp. 157–63.

Page 1 Pigalle Plato shoe
by Christian Louboutin;
see pp. 43–48.

**Page 2 (left to right, from
top row)** Birkenstock;
Camilla Skovgaard;
Camper; Charles Jourdan;
Charlotte Olympia;
Christian Louboutin;
Church's; Clarks; Converse;
Salvatore Ferragamo;
Havaianas; Gina; Camper;
Gil Carvalho; Jimmy Choo.

**Page 3 (left to right, from
top row)** Kurt Geiger;
Manolo Blahnik; Melissa;
Pierre Hardy; Manolo
Blahnik; Pretty Ballerinas;
Repetto; Robert Clergerie;
Roger Vivier; Rupert
Sanderson; Swedish
Hasbeens; Terry de Havilland;
Tod's; Nicholas Kirkwood.

Page 4 Gili shoe by Robert
Clergerie; see pp. 139–43.

First published in 2012 by Merrell Publishers,
London and New York

Merrell Publishers Limited
81 Southwark Street
London SE1 0HX

merrellpublishers.com

British Library Cataloguing-in-Publication data:
Walker, Harriet, 1985–
Cult shoes : classic and contemporary designs.
1. Women's shoes. 2. Women's shoes – History.
3. Women's shoes – Design.
I. Title
391.4′13′082-DC23

ISBN 978-1-8589-4585-9

Produced by Merrell Publishers Limited
Designed by Alexandre Coco
Project-managed by Rosanna Lewis
Indexed by Hilary Bird

Printed and bound in China

9 781858 945859